BLENDED QUILT
BACKGROUNDS

Create Secondary Patterns

JEAN BIDDICK

American Quilter's Society

P. O. Box 3290 • Paducah, KY 42002-3290
FAX 270-898-1173 *www.americanquilter.com*

Located in Paducah, Kentucky, the American Quilter's Society (AQS) is dedicated to promoting the accomplishments of today's quilters. Through its publications and events, AQS strives to honor today's quiltmakers and their work and to inspire future creativity and innovation in quiltmaking.

EDITOR: SHELLEY HAWKINS
GRAPHIC DESIGN: AMY CHASE
COVER DESIGN: MICHAEL BUCKINGHAM
PHOTOGRAPHY: CHARLES R. LYNCH

Library of Congress Cataloging-in-Publication Data
Biddick, Jean.
    Blended quilt backgrounds / by Jean Biddick.
    p. cm.
Summary: "Transform traditional block designs to reshape into newly formed backgrounds. Author leads you through the process with step-by-step, clear instructions helping you create a new look for traditional block designs. Includes many tips to help new and experienced quilters refine their piecing skills"-- Provided by publisher.
  ISBN 978-1-57432-929-2
1. Patchwork--Patterns. 2. Quilting--Patterns. 3. Patchwork quilts. I. Title.

TT835.B48145 2007
746.46'041--dc22
                        2007001199

Additional copies of this book may be ordered from the American Quilter's Society, PO Box 3290, Paducah, KY 42002-3290; 800-626-5420 (orders only please); or online at www.AmericanQuilter.com. For all other inquiries, please call 270-898-7903.

Cover Quilt: CARIBBEAN HOLIDAY (page 27), made by the author and quilted by Mary Vaneecke

DEDICATION

In memory of my mother, Lois Seyfrit, who taught me to sew and gave me my first quilting book.

ACKNOWLEDGMENTS

Thank you to

Jeff Biddick, Kathy Bower, Jo Cady-Bull
Sherall Donovan, Jeanne Fraser,
Brooke Miller, Kathleen Nitzsche,
Gayle Strack, and Jo Ann Strohn
for sharing their quilts,

Terry Clark, Jo Lee Hazelwood,
and Mary Vaneecke
for quilting my quilts,

Pam Ashbaugh, Linn Lindley,
and Mary McLaughlin
for testing patterns,

Shelley Hawkins
for editing the book,

Amy Chase
for designing the book,

Members of Sunset Quilters Bee
for their encouragement and support,

All my students
for their enthusiasm, and

My husband, Chris
for his love.

CONTENTS

INTRODUCTION

When my son was leaving for college, he asked for a quilt for his dorm room – a request any mother would be thrilled to honor. I planned an Ohio Star design with a variety of plaid flannels for the stars and many beige and tan fabrics for the background. My original plan was to scatter the beiges throughout the background, but when placing fabrics on the design wall, I found that the background was too busy and the stars were getting lost.

There were several choices at that point. I could use just one beige background fabric. I could still use a variety of background fabrics, but make them all closer in value to the lightest fabric. I could make the background from all solid or nearly solid fabrics so it did not compete with the plaids. I also wondered what would happen if all these different background fabrics were organized instead of scattered throughout the quilt.

By placing tracing paper over the original layout, I experimented with different divisions of the background areas. A progression of light to dark beige and brown fabrics behind the stars began to take shape. The plaid flannel stars seemed much happier when placed on an organized background. The final result was PLENTIFUL PLAIDS, a quilt my son has enjoyed for over a decade.

Shading the background of the whole quilt instead of just using one fabric or color family for the entire background opens many new possibilities for quilt design.

PLENTIFUL PLAIDS, 68" x 104". Quilt made by the author for her son, Jeff Biddick.

The two designs on this page are made with the same blocks. The only difference between the designs is in the background coloring. In the first design, the entire background is white (fig. 1). In the second, some of the background is black and some yellow-green (fig. 2). The resulting design is much more interesting.

When I started shading the backgrounds of my quilts from light to dark, I wasn't thinking of the other things that could be done with this idea. Each project opened new areas to explore and a lot of "what would happen if…" conversations in my head.

What if the background colors didn't make a progression from light to dark, but instead emphasized different background areas?

What if the foreground areas were also colored on the whole quilt instead of block by block?

What if the warm and cool colors were traded? Would the background become the foreground?

What if some of the background areas were colored the same as the foreground?

By looking behind the scenes and paying attention to the background areas of the blocks, you can design incredibly interesting new quilts.

Fig. 1. This quilt has interesting shapes, but the coloring does not make a very exciting quilt.

Fig. 2. A black background in the outer areas and a yellow-green background near the center enhance the design.

DESIGN BASICS

Fig. 1. These blocks are not easy to work with. The first has too many pieces that are the same. The second has a very large center square that takes up too much of the design area.

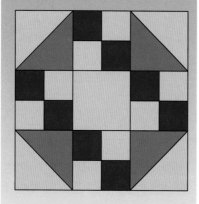

Fig. 2. This block offers more design opportunities. It has different-shaped pieces and includes strong diagonal lines that provide an easy way to add lines in the background.

There are three basic steps in designing your own blended background quilt.

Step 1: Choose a Block

Some blocks are easier to work with than others (fig. 1). A block that includes diagonal lines offers the simplest way to add seams in the background (fig. 2). Blocks that contain more than one shape or the same shape in more than one size offer multiple coloring opportunities.

Step 2: Draw the Layout

You will need to start with a vague idea of your finished quilt size. Because you will color the entire quilt at once, it is difficult to expand the design by adding more blocks after coloring. However, you can vary your quilt size by making larger blocks or adding more borders. You are always allowed to change your mind, but be aware that adding blocks to your design will be the most difficult way to make a change.

When you decide on the number of blocks, you need to draw enough blocks to fill the quilt layout. There are several choices for this step. You can draw the block on graph paper and repeat it as many times as necessary. You can make one drawing and use a copy machine to make additional copies that can be cut out and pasted together. However, copy machines do not always make accurately sized copies and blocks may not fit together perfectly.

Quilt design software can make short work of drawing the quilt layout. If you use a computer, this may be the easiest way to start your design. Multiple copies of the block can be made quickly, and when you are ready to color your design, the process of trying out different colors goes much faster.

Step 3: Color and Adjust the Design

Here is the fun part. There are several options for coloring your design.

1. Start with a simple line drawing that has no shading to distinguish the foreground from the background. This is not the easiest way to begin, but offers the most freedom.

2. Use shades of gray to fill the foreground. This makes it easier to see the difference between the leading actors and supporting cast, allowing you to work on the background without getting it confused with the foreground.

3. Use color to show distinction between the foreground and background. When using only gray-scale to delineate the foreground, it's tempting to use too many different background colors. Assigning all warm or all cool colors to the foreground areas can be helpful. You can then use the opposite set of colors for the background. What you need are several values for both the foreground and background. It is actually the contrast in values, not the different colors, that makes the design come alive.

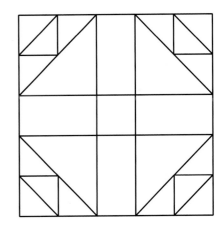

Fig. 3. Duck and Ducklings block

Once the foreground is shaded, colored, or left as a line drawing, it is time to decide how to use those background supporting areas to make your quilt sing. You can start coloring the background or add more lines so you have more coloring choices. When drawing new divisions, you do not have to color adjacent patches differently. Those seams can always be removed from the final design. Right now, you are just auditioning shapes and designs to isolate in the quilt.

Some possible variations in coloring your background are to color it without adding more lines, add dividing lines to the background, or use a line drawing without shading in the foreground. The best way to understand the blended background technique is through a sample project. The Duck and Ducklings block is used to illustrate the technique (fig. 3).

Fig. 4. The four gray-scale blocks could be compared to preparing for a play. The script is ready, but the actors have not yet been hired.

Our sample is a small wallhanging with just four blocks (fig. 4). Secondary patterns emerge when the blocks are placed next to each other.

Fig. 5. The lead actors are hired by filling in the foreground with warm colors.

Fig. 6. The supporting actors are hired by coloring the background with two shades of blue. This version emphasizes the quilt's square center.

The blocks (fig. 4, on page 9) are in gray scale to illustrate the difference between the foreground and background areas. Before working with the background, it can be helpful to replace the gray scale with color. For our example, warm colors are used in the foreground (fig. 5).

The background areas in this first example are colored without adding any extra seam lines. Cool colors for the background in at least two different values are shown (figs. 6–7).

This is the simplest version of the technique. Let's explore some variations.

Variation 1

This time, before coloring the background, we will add some more lines in the background areas. Adding these lines greatly increases our design possibilities (fig. 8). It is easiest to add lines that follow some of the original lines of the block. If lines are added at new angles, piecing becomes more difficult. Adding lines that extend existing ones is a much better plan.

Fig. 7. Using the supporting actors in different roles, a grid is emphasized that makes the quilt look like it was made of smaller blocks with a light blue sashing.

Fig. 8. The background areas of the four blocks are divided into more pieces. Perhaps the budget was expanded and more supporting actors were hired.

Auditioning Design Possibilities

Use tracing paper to audition different ideas. Add lines and test coloring options on the tracing paper. Each new idea for background divisions and coloring schemes can be done on a separate sheet of tracing paper, eliminating the need to continually redraw the block layout.

After adding lines, try different ways of coloring the background. Every patch does not need to be a different color (fig. 9). Some adjacent patches use the same fabric coloring. At this point, you are just highlighting parts of the design. Figure 10 shows another possible coloring.

Don't limit yourself to just one way of adding lines to the base drawing. Use a new piece of tracing paper to add different lines to the background areas and to audition new coloring schemes (figs. 11–13).

Fig. 9. More supporting actors have been hired and their roles determined.

Fig. 10. This coloring shows a different way the actors' roles could be distributed.

Fig. 11. A new director for the play has a different idea of the supporting actors' roles.

Fig. 12. The new director has assigned roles to the supporting cast.

Fig. 13. After a few rehearsals, the director changed the way he distributed the roles.

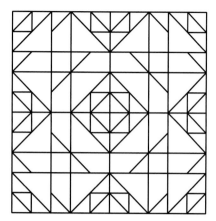

Fig. 14. This is a line drawing of the quilt without color.

Fig. 15. When hiring the actors, we are looking for an ensemble cast without any big-name stars.

Fig. 16. This is another way to assign ensemble cast roles.

Variation 2

Another variation is to start with just a line drawing that has no foreground shading. Again, we can add new lines and experiment with colorings. New shapes are found as we color the design. By not making a difference between the original foreground and background areas we open up even more design possibilities.

Figure 14 shows the same design as figure 8, but without the shading. This time we can color the entire quilt and see the shapes relate to each other in different ways (fig. 15). Figure 16 shows another possible coloring.

Variation 3

Choosing a block that is symmetric along the diagonal is another way to begin your design. The Road to Oklahoma block has the strong diagonal symmetry that works well in this variation (fig. 17). The blocks can be set by turning every other block 90° (fig. 18).

Variation 4

Another variation is to use two different blocks. Choosing blocks based on different grids makes piecing easier because you will not have to match seam intersections when the blocks are

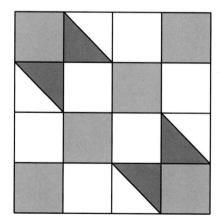

Fig. 17. Road to Oklahoma block

sewn together. Another asset to this variation is that you seldom need to add more lines to the backgrounds. There is usually enough variety without them (fig. 19).

Fig. 18. The blocks are set with every other block rotated by 90° and colored as an ensemble cast.

Fig. 19. An Ohio Star and an Album block are used alternately in this setting. The coloring was done with a very large ensemble cast in mind.

Design Practice

Explore design possibilities in the following examples (figs. 20–22). Each quilt is presented as an outline drawing with a block(s) shown in gray scale to highlight the foreground areas of the original block. Use tracing paper over the designs or photocopy and enlarge them to try out your ideas. Design ideas can be tested on the entire layout or limited to fewer blocks. The choice is up to you.

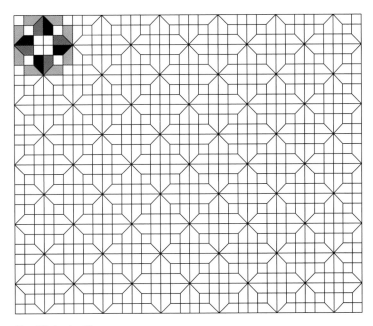

Fig. 20. Lucky Clover

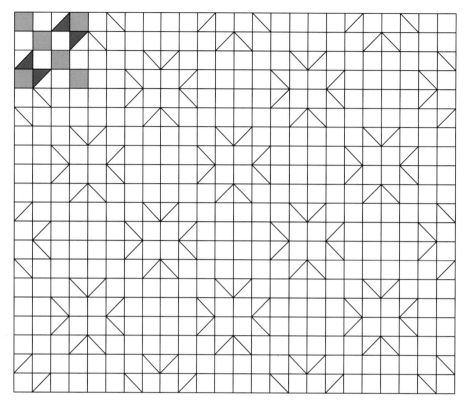

Fig. 21. Road to Oklahoma

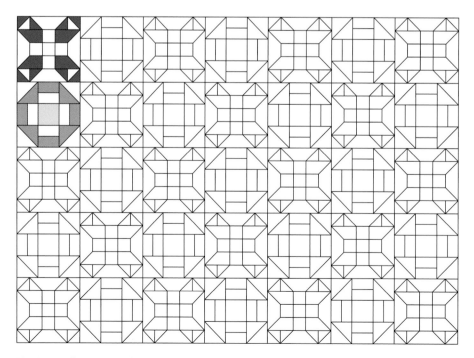

Fig. 22. Fool's Square and Grecian Square

PLANNING YOUR QUILT

Planning the Piecing

Once you decide on a design for your quilt, it is time to plan the piecing. Each project is different and the piecing plan needs to be specific. Piecing the quilt block by block is not always the best choice because it often means including more seams than necessary.

The first step in planning the piecing is to remove any lines that are between two identical fabrics. *You can see the way the pieces fit together by forgetting about the block being the basis of your design.* There will be places where the fabric flows across lines in the original block structure and could be cut as one large piece. On the other hand, some areas may create such odd shapes that they need to be divided to facilitate piecing. To illustrate this concept, one of the previous designs is shown without the seam lines (fig. 1).

Make a few copies of the design without seam lines. Then get out your scissors and see where the design can be cut apart. You may find it easiest to cut it into rows (fig. 2) or into sections (fig. 3).

We will use the second option as we continue to plan our quilt. There is one large center, four identical corners, and four identical side sections (fig. 4, page 16).

Fig. 1. This design has the seam lines removed between the blocks.

Fig. 2. The design could be cut into rows.

OR

Fig. 3. The design could be cut into sections.

Corner section

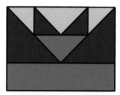

Side section

Center section

Fig. 4. The three basic sections of our design.

a

b

c

Fig. 5. Piecing plan for the (a) center section, (b) corner sections, and (c) side sections

Determining Shapes and Sizes

Once piecing is planned, a cutting chart can be made to determine how much fabric is needed. The first decision is the size of the quilt or of the base block. The Duck and Ducklings block is based on a five-by-five grid, so any multiple of five will be a good size.

If the block is 10" square, it will make the quilt 20" square, and the smallest piece in the quilt will finish to a 2" square. That seems like a smaller quilt than we would like. If we make the block size 15", our smallest piece will be 3" square and our quilt will be 30" square. That seems like a better size. Look at the basic sections and see how each one can be pieced (fig. 5). Make a list of the pieces that need to be cut for each section. This initial list uses the finished size of each piece.

Corner section (make four)
One 3" yellow square
One 3" red half-square triangle
Five 3" dark blue half-square triangles
One 6" red half-square triangle
Two light blue trapezoids (one reverse)

Side section (make four)
Two 3" light blue half-square triangles
Two 3" red half-square triangles
Two 6" red half-square triangles
One 6" dark blue quarter-square triangle
One 6" light blue quarter-square triangle
One 3" x 12" rectangle

Center section (make one)
Four 6" red half-square triangles
Four 3" red half-square triangles
Four 6" light blue quarter-square triangles
One dark blue on-point square

Translating to Cut Sizes

Organize the pieces identified for all of the sections and make a list of all the different pieces in the quilt. List the largest pieces first.

Finished Sizes

6" quarter-square triangle
6" half-square triangle
3" x 12" rectangle
3" x 6" trapezoid
on-point square
3" half-square triangle
3" square

How big should I cut the pieces?

Squares: Add ½" to the finished size.
Rectangles: Add ½" to each dimension.
Half-square Triangles: Add ⅞" to the finished edge.
Quarter-square Triangles: Add 1¼" to the finished edge.
On-point squares, trapezoids and other unusual shapes: Draw the exact shape, add ¼" seam allowances, and make a template.

Make a Cutting Chart

After determining the size to cut each piece, you will need to make a cutting chart (fig. 6). Adding a symbol to remind yourself which pieces are the squares, half-square triangles, quarter-square triangles, etc. is helpful. Use the information from the cutting chart to decide how much fabric is needed for each part of your quilt.

Shape & Size	Number of Pieces to Cut			
Fabric →	1	2	3	4
⊠ A – 7¼"			2 (8)	1 (4)
◩ B – 6⅞"		8 (16)		
⊤ C – 4¾"				1
◩ D – 3⅞"		8 (16)	4 (8)	10 (20)
▭ E – 3½" x 12½"				4
⊤ F – 3½" x 6⅞"			4 & 4r	
□ G – 3½"	4			

Fig. 6. Cutting Chart

Piecing Tips and Techniques

There are many things that can make a difference to the success of your project. The fabric, thread, cutting, and sewing machine all play a part in precision piecing. Each step of the process has variables that can improve or sabotage your perfect points.

Fabric

Use the best quality fabric you can afford. Good-quality fabric increases your chances for success. Poor quality will just make you frustrated. Fabrics that feel like cardboard or fabrics that have no body at all will make your job more difficult.

Another decision is whether or not to prewash the fabric. Neither choice is right or wrong. I prefer prewashing because it removes the chemicals used in the finishing process and gets rid of most of the excess dye. Fabrics come with different amounts of sizing, and washing them first makes them more similar in feel to each other and they tend to behave in a more uniform manner.

Cutting

Using the plain side of your cutting mat can increase your accuracy. The problem with the marked side is that you are aligning three things: the fabric, the lines on the mat, and the ruler. It is easy to have one of them off a bit. On the plain side, you can align the ruler with the folded edge of the fabric. Now there are only two things that need to be in alignment instead of three. The result is a more accurate cut.

Templates

Many shapes can be cut with just a measurement on the ruler, but a few need to be done with a template.

The temptation is to make the template, then place the ruler over the template to do the cutting. It is difficult to get the ruler positioned exactly right. It is easy to cut off a sliver of the template, making it inaccurate. Instead, try butting the ruler against the template edge.

First, place rolled pieces of masking tape on the bottom of the template so it will stay in place. Put the ruler on the fabric, but not on the template (fig. 1). Slide the ruler up to the edge of the template so it is a snug fit. The rotary cutter is thin enough to fit between the ruler and the template without cutting away the template material.

Sewing Machine

The more familiar you are with the way your machine works, the more successful you will be. Keep it clean, lint free, and oiled. A happy machine will give you many hours of comfortable sewing. A poorly maintained machine will make your life miserable.

Use good thread and make sure your needle is a good match for the thread. Piecing is generally done with 100% cotton thread in a 50/3 size. The needle size needs to match the thread size. For this thread, the best matches are a Microtex needle in size 70/10

Fig. 1. Placing the ruler against the edge of the template works better than placing the ruler on top of the template.

or 80/12, or a quilting needle in size 75/11. The bevel on these needles pierces the fabric and keeps stitches straighter than a Universal needle.

Changing the throat plate from the normal wide-hole plate to a single-hole can also make straighter stitches. The wide hole accommodates the zigzag, but is not helpful when sewing straight seams.

The presser foot you choose can affect your accuracy. There are many varieties and styles of feet. The standard foot on many machines includes a solid or nearly solid bar across the foot that obstructs your view (fig. 2a). Most machines offer a foot that measures ¼" from the needle to the edge of the foot (figs. 2b–c). These feet give you a reasonably good guide, but you should test them before relying on their accuracy. A

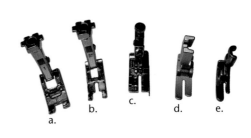

Fig. 2. Presser feet

straight-stitch foot (figs. 2d–e) is narrower than ¼". You will not be able to use the foot as your ¼" guide, but you have more control of the fabric and can hold it as you finish sewing right up to the end of your seam.

Accurate Seam

Piecing is done with a ¼" seam. It is important to locate and test the ¼" seam allowance on your machine. One way to test is with an index card. Most standard cards have lines that are exactly ¼" apart. Use your ruler to make sure.

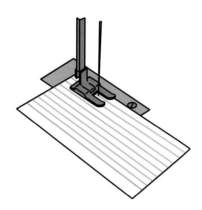

Fig. 3. Sewing on the line of the index card is one way to test a ¼" seam.

Trim the card on one of the lines, then sew on the line next to the trimmed edge. Sew for about 1" and be sure that the needle is hitting the line at each stitch (fig. 3). If the edge of the card is exactly at the edge of the foot, you have an accurate ¼" foot. If it aligns with a mark on the throat plate or the edge of the foot, you have a good guide for a ¼" seam. If the card does not align with anything, you can establish a guide with masking tape. Choose a tape that contrasts with the color of the bed of your machine, such as blue painter's tape. Place the tape along the card edge and closer to your body than the feed dogs. Do not cover part of the feeding mechanism.

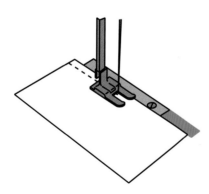

Fig. 4. Sew on the blank side of the index card to test your stitching guide.

To test your guide, turn the index card over so you can no longer see the lines. Align the cut edge of the card with your established guide and sew again for about 1" (fig. 4). Remove the card from the machine and turn it over. If the stitches are on the line, you have successfully found a ¼" guide.

Construction

It is much easier to learn accurate piecing techniques than it is to continually pick out seams and resew them. There are many shapes that are used repeatedly in piecing. Here are a few suggestions for handling some of them.

Half-square triangles

Using a paper foundation makes very accurate triangle pairs, but after sewing, you have to cut the paper pieces apart and remove the paper. That takes a lot of time.

Drawing a line down the diagonal of a pair of squares also takes time because you have to cut the pairs apart one at a time after they have been sewn.

I prefer to cut accurate triangles and just sew the seams. The cutting takes less time because I am cutting four layers at once, and cutting accurately means no trimming to size after pressing. Learning to handle the bias edge is not that difficult. Just remind yourself to treat it gently.

Start at the right angle when aligning the triangle pairs (fig. 5). That way, if the diagonal cut is even a tiny bit off, the two sides of the square will match exactly.

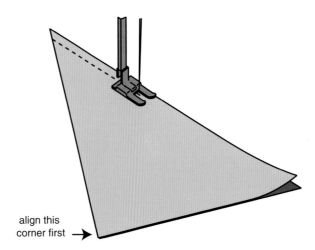

align this corner first →

Fig. 5. This half-square triangle pair is aligned and sewn along the long edge.

Square-in-a-Square

There are three steps that make these units more accurate:

1. Fold the square and the triangles to find the center of each piece. Match the centers and pin the first two triangles on opposite sides of the square. Make sure that the overlap of the tips form a square (fig. 6). If they form a rectangle, they are not lined up properly.

2. Make an ironing template with muslin and a permanent marker. Draw a square that is ½" larger than the finished size of the unit you are making. Press the two triangles away from the center square using the ironing template. When pressing the triangles, be sure they fit exactly into opposite corners of the ironing template (fig. 7, page 22). This helps avoid overstretching the unit. Do not trim the points yet.

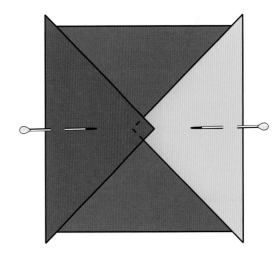

Fig. 6. Notice the center where the tips of the triangles form a square.

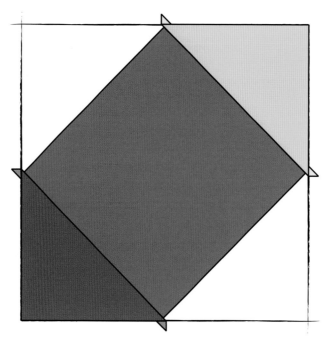

Fig. 7. The triangles are pressed to fit perfectly in the corners of the ironing template.

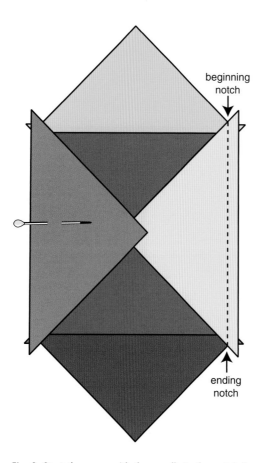

beginning
notch

ending
notch

3. Align and pin the remaining triangles to opposite sides of the square. Check the overlapping tips to be sure they form a square. Start and stop your sewing line exactly in the notch formed at the edge of the triangle (fig. 8). Lowering the needle and placing the notch against it helps start the seam correctly. Use the pressing template again to make sure the unit is the right size. Trim the points to reduce bulk.

Fig. 8. Start the seam with the needle in the notch formed at the unit's edge.

If you add more triangles to this unit, it is easiest to sew with the new triangles on the bottom and the square with its first four triangles on top (fig. 9). This allows you to see where the threads cross on the back of the unit, and you can be sure your line of stitching hits that intersection.

Flying Geese

Large Flying Geese

The large triangle is cut as a quarter-square triangle and the two smaller triangles are cut as half-square triangles. The result is a unit with outer edges that fall on the straight grain of fabric.

Start with the point of the large triangle away from you and sew a small triangle to the right side, aligning edges perfectly (fig. 10). Press the seam allowance toward the small triangle. The second triangle also aligns perfectly with the edges of the large triangle and a notch is formed where the two small triangles meet. Your sewing line needs to end exactly in the notch (fig. 11).

Small Flying Geese

The folded corner technique is used for small Flying Geese. Instead of cutting three triangles, cut a rectangle and two squares. Fold each square or mark the diagonal. Place one square on the rectangle,

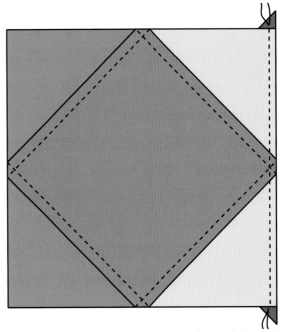

Fig. 9. Being able to see where the threads cross helps with accuracy.

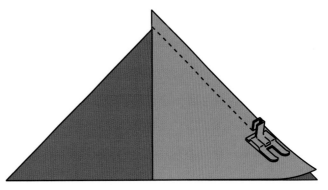

Fig. 10. The first triangle is added to the Flying Geese unit.

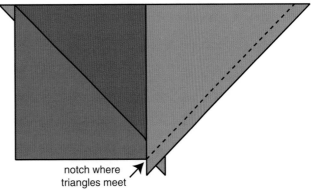

notch where triangles meet

Fig. 11. When sewing the second triangle, be sure to end at the notch.

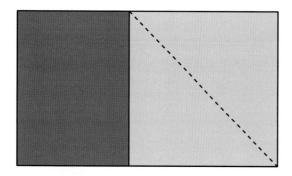

Fig. 12. The diagonal of the small square is used as a sewing guide for this unit.

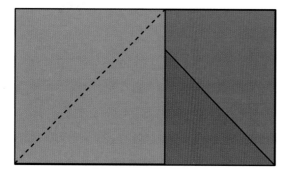

Fig. 13. Align the second square and sew on the diagonal.

carefully aligning the edges (fig. 12). Sew on the diagonal. Fold the corner of the square and press so it aligns exactly with the original rectangle edges. Unfold the corner and place the ¼" mark of the ruler on the seam line. Cut away the two fabric layers at the corner. Add the other square in the same manner, making sure the diagonal crosses the first seam (fig. 13).

Units like 54-40 or Fight

The long, skinny triangles in the 54-40 or Fight type of block can be difficult to align with the central triangle. When making the templates, you will notice that the tip of the skinny triangle has been trimmed. When the small triangle is placed on the large triangle, the trimmed corner helps with alignment (fig. 14). When the second triangle is added, the alignment includes a small notch (fig. 15). Both the notch and trimmed corner of the small triangle can help align the pieces.

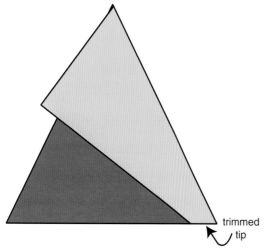

Fig. 14. The pieces of the 54-40 or Fight unit align perfectly at the trimmed tip of the skinny triangle.

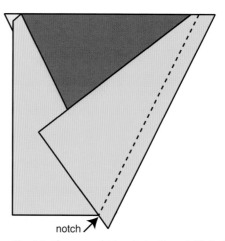

Fig. 15. The second triangle is aligned. Notice the notch at the bottom edge of the seam.

Pinning

After the units have been sewn, they are often joined into rows and there are places that the seams from two adjacent rows need to be matched. Good-quality pins improve the accuracy of your piecing. Look for silk pins that are 1¼" long and have a shaft diameter of .50 mm. These pins go into the fabric easily, are long enough to hold the fabric firmly, and are thin enough to sew over.

If an intersection contains only square corners, press the seam allowances in opposite directions and use the ridge that is formed to help align the seams. Once the ridges are meshed, a pin placed just to the left of the seam line holds the pieces in place while they are sewn and keeps the seam allowance from getting caught and flipped in the wrong direction. If you place a pin exactly on the seam, it will push the pieces out of alignment. Placing the pin just to the left of the seam will hold down the seam allowance that goes through the machine first (fig. 16).

If a triangle point is at an intersection, you need to be more careful in pinning. For this type of match, you need three pins. The first is inserted exactly at the point along each seam you want to match. While the pin keeps the fabrics aligned, use two other pins to anchor the pieces so they do not shift. After inserting the two anchoring pins, the positioning pin can stay in as a marker or be removed. If there is an X of thread where the positioning pin went in, it can be removed. If not, leave this pin as a marker. The thread X or the pin is used as a sewing guide to produce a precise point (fig 17).

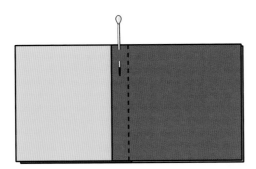

Fig. 16. A plain intersection is pinned to the left of the seam.

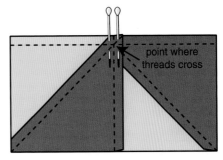

point where threads cross

Fig. 17. Pinning for an intersection that includes at least one point

QUILT PROJECTS

Cut a square

Cut a square once
diagonally

Cut a square twice
diagonally

Cut a rectangle

Use the template
provided

Each of the projects includes information about the block or blocks that form the basis of the quilt. The size of the base block and quilt is listed, even if the quilt is not constructed in a block-by-block style.

The cutting charts are organized so that the largest pieces are listed first. Start by cutting a strip the size of the first piece. Cut the pieces required for that size. If there is enough of the strip left, trim it to the next smallest size and continue cutting pieces. This allows you to make the best use of your fabrics.

The sidebar contains a key for the symbols in the cutting charts. For half-square and quarter-square triangles, the first number in the cutting chart indicates how many squares to cut. The number in parentheses indicates how many triangles are used in the project. Templates are provided with each project for shapes such as trapezoids and on-point squares.

CARIBBEAN HOLIDAY

Base block size: 9" • Quilt size: 54" x 63"
Made by the author and quilted by Mary Vaneecke

Ohio Star blocks with a blending of values in the background make for a tropical celebration. The quilt is pieced in wide and narrow rows instead of individual blocks.

Yardage

Yardage is based on a 40" width.

Placement	Fabric	Yards
Stars & inner border		total of ten fabrics– ¼ of five and ⅜ of five
Background	1	¼
	2	½
	3	½
	4	⅝
	5	¾
	6	½
Outer border & binding		2
Backing*		3¼

*crosswise seam

Cutting Chart

Refer to the symbol key on page 26. An "r" indicates that a template needs to be reversed. Templates are on pages 33–34.

Shape & Size				Number of Pieces to Cut				
Fabric →	Star	1	2	3	4	5	6
☐ A – 6½"			2	2	2	5	
T B – template			1	3	4		1
⊠ C – 4¼"	6 (24)*	2 (8)	6 (22)	8 (31)	8 (29)	9 (34)	4 (16)
◣ D – 3⅞"		1 (1)	2 (3)			4 (7)	
▭ E – 3½" x 6½"		2	4	2	2	4	2
T F – template							1 & 1r
☐ G – 3½"	3*	1		1	1		1
☐ H – 2⅝"		2	10	9	8	18	2

*Cut this amount from each star fabric.

Construction

When laying out the pieces, you may find yourself trying to make actual Ohio Star blocks, but after the first few sections, you will start to see a different pattern. There is always a small square on point that links one star to the next.

1. Decide on the placement of the star fabric for the 30 blocks. Each fabric is used for three stars. Arrange only the center squares of the star fabrics in a 5 x 6 grid.

2. Starting at the upper left, lay out the first few stars, then fill in with the background pieces. Refer to the background fabric guide, page 29, to see where the fabrics change.

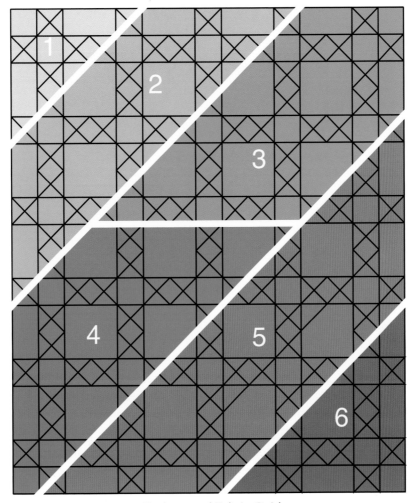

Background Fabric Guide

3. Refer to the unit assembly guides to piece 22 of unit 1 and 49 of unit 2, paying close attention to the fabric placement in the layout. The pressing is different depending on the orientation of the unit. The arrows on the pressing guide, page 30, show the direction to press the seam allowances.

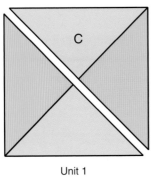

Unit 1
make 22

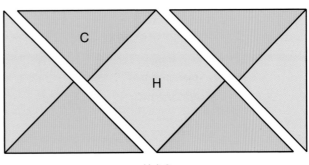

Unit 2
make 49

Following the pressing guide will result in opposing seams when the units are joined to each other.

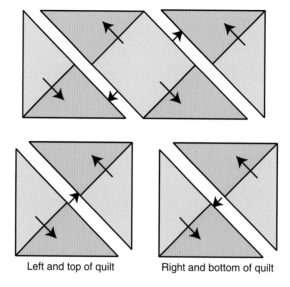

Left and top of quilt   Right and bottom of quilt

Pressing Guide

4. There are a few places where the large background square needs to be pieced from a large triangle and template 1, and there are a few places around the edge where the rectangle is made from a triangle and template 2. The seams for these sections are sometimes pressed toward the triangle and sometimes away. Look at the adjoining sections to decide how to press.

5. After the units are pieced, refer to the quilt assembly diagram, page 31, to join the units and remaining squares to form 13 rows. Join the rows.

Borders
Inner Border Cutting Chart
Cut rectangles as indicated in the chart. Refer to the quilt assembly diagram, page 31, and cut the appropriate 45° angle at the ends of each rectangle.

Shape & Size	Number of Pieces to Cut				
Fabric →	1	2	3	4	5
☐ I – 1½" x 18¼"	2				
☐ J – 1½" x 20¼"		2			
☐ K – 1½" x 23¼"			1	2	
☐ L – 1½" x 14¼"			2		
☐ M – 1½" x 5¼"			1		
☐ N – 1½" x 24¼"					2

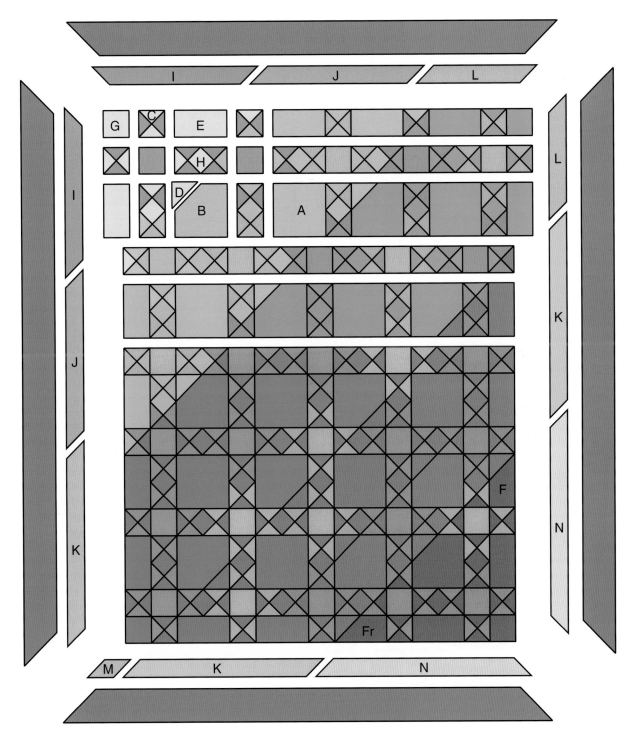

Quilt Assembly

1. The inner border is pieced from narrow strips of five of the star fabrics. All of the angled cuts in the border will match a place where the background fabrics have changed. The backgrounds change value from light to dark. The border fabrics change value from dark to light. Refer to the quilt assembly diagram, page 31, to add the inner border.

2. For the outer border, cut four lengthwise strips 4" x 65" each. Measure the edges of your quilt top. Measure and attach the border strips. Mark the 45° angle, sew the mitered corner, and trim the excess.

3. Quilt the layers and bind.

Kathleen Nitzsche of Plainfield, New Jersey, used a larger Ohio Star when she made THERE IS NO STOPPING ME NOW. The subtle shading within the fabrics adds interest and movement.

Brooke Miller of Tucson, Arizona, used just one fabric for the stars. The result is a quilt in which the background is more important than the stars. LOST STARS is a good example of how fabric choices create an entirely different pattern.

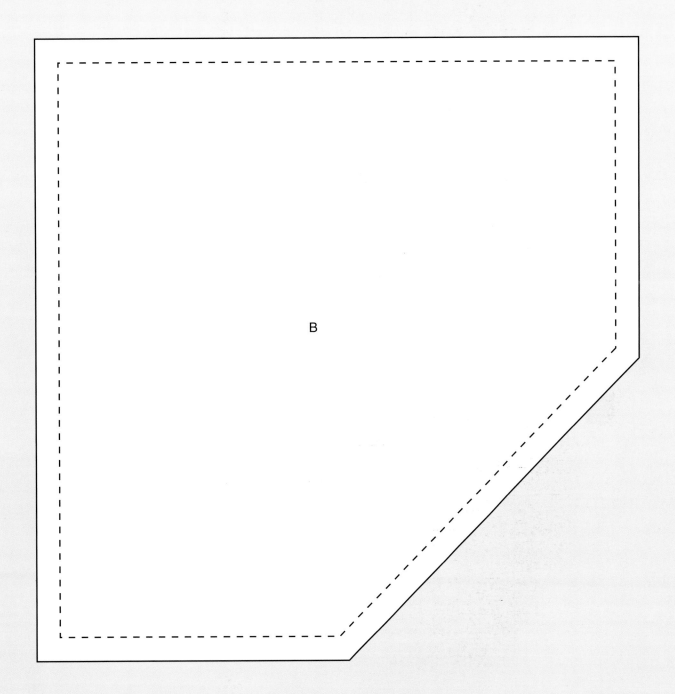

B

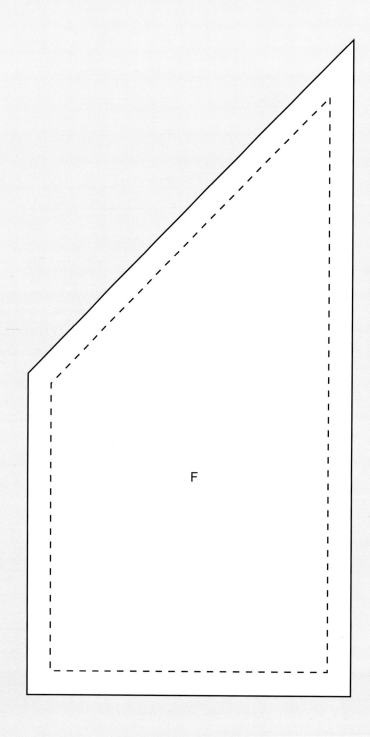

F

CASTLE WALLS

Base block size: 8" • Quilt size: 56" x 56"
Made by the author and quilted by Mary Vaneecke

In this quilt, the traditional Crosses and Losses block was set in a 6 x 6 grid with alternate blocks turned 90°. The quilt was colored to emphasize bands of fabric around the central motif. It reminds me of the central keep of a castle surrounded by walls and battlements.

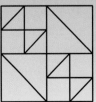

Yardage

Yardage is based on a 40" width.

Placement	Fabric	Yards
Units & border triangles	1	¾
Units & border	2	1½
Units	3	⅝
	4	½
	5	½
Units, border & binding	6	1¼
Units	7	⅜
	8	⅝
Backing		3⅓

Cutting Chart

Before cutting the following pieces, cut eight light blue strips 3" x 29¼" from fabric 2 and eight dark rust strips 2" x 29¼" from fabric 6 for the borders. Templates are on page 39.

Shape & Size	Number of Pieces to Cut							
Fabric →	1	2	3	4	5	6	7	8
⊠ A – 9¼"	1 (4)	2 (8)		1 (4)				
⊠ B – 5¼"	3 (12)	2 (8)		2 (8)				
◹ C – 4⅞"						24 (48)	12 (24)	
☐ D – 3⅜"		4	8	1	4			
Ⓣ E – template	8				8			
⊠ F – 3¼"		2 (8)						
◹ G – 2⅞"	12 (24)	18 (36)	8 (16)	2 (4)	6 (12)	4 (8)		68 (136)
☐ H – 2½"	16	16		8	24			
▭ I – 2½" x 4½"		24	32	4				
Ⓣ J – template				4				

Construction

The piecing for this quilt is done in rows instead of in blocks with a variety of different units. In the units, you will see one shape repeated many times, which looks like a Flying Geese unit with only one wing. These sections are constructed with the folded corner technique (see Small Flying Geese, pages 23–24). Make the units on the following page:

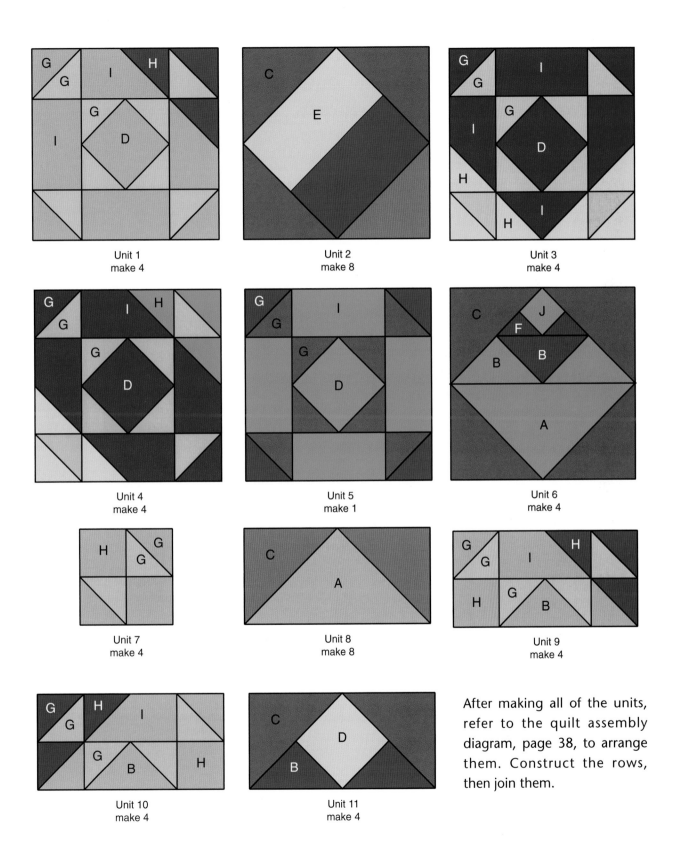

Unit 1
make 4

Unit 2
make 8

Unit 3
make 4

Unit 4
make 4

Unit 5
make 1

Unit 6
make 4

Unit 7
make 4

Unit 8
make 8

Unit 9
make 4

Unit 10
make 4

Unit 11
make 4

After making all of the units, refer to the quilt assembly diagram, page 38, to arrange them. Construct the rows, then join them.

Quilt Assembly

Borders

Join a blue strip to a rust strip. Cut a 45° angle at each end, leaving the blue fabric the longest. Repeat for the remaining strips. Join two of these sections with one of the dark blue 9¼" triangles to make each border. Add the borders to the quilt, mitering the corners. Quilt the layers and bind.

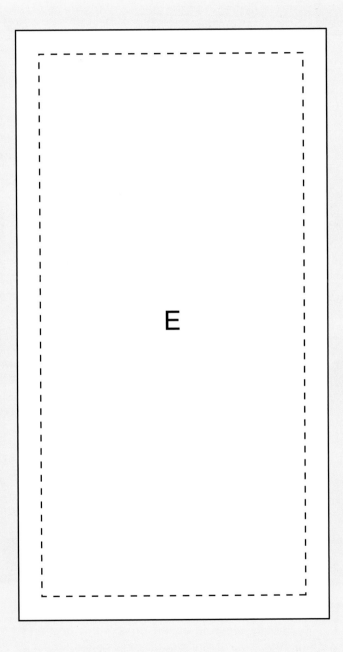

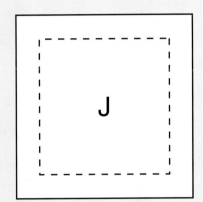

Spring Garden

Base block size: 7½" • Quilt size: 46" x 46"
Made and quilted by the author

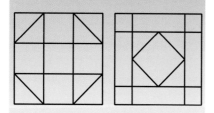

This wallhanging combines two traditional blocks. The Shoofly block is based on a 3 x 3 grid and the Album block on a 5 x 5 grid. This makes piecing especially easy because there are no intersections to match when the blocks are joined. The quilt was colored as an ensemble cast with no leading actors.

Yardage

Yardage is based on a 40" width.

Placement	Fabric	Yards
Blocks & outer border	1	1⅜
	2	½
	3	¾
Blocks & inner border	4	⅜
	5	½
	6	½
Backing & binding		3

Cutting Chart

Before cutting the following pieces, cut two strips 3½" x 40½" and two strips 3½" x 46½" across the length of fabric 1 for the outer border.

Then, cut two strips 1¾" x 38" and two strips 1¾" x 40½" across the width of fabric 4 for the inner border.

Shape & Size	Number of Pieces to Cut					
Fabric →	1	2	3	4	5	6
☐ A – 3⅝"	1				12	
◨ B – 3⅜"	8 (16)	24 (48)	4 (8)		4 (8)	8 (16)
◨ C – 3⅛"	2 (4)	6 (12)	4 (8)	2 (4)		12 (24)
☐ D – 3"		12	32	16		
☐ E – 2" x 5"	4		28		20	
☐ F – 2"	20		8			24

Construction

1. The Album block consists of a Square-in-a-Square with borders. Refer to the tips on pages 21–23 to construct the center. Arrows in the diagram on page 42 show the seam allowance pressing direction.

2. The Shoofly block is made with four pairs of half-square triangles and five squares. Press the seam allowances of the triangle units toward the corners. Make the following blocks:

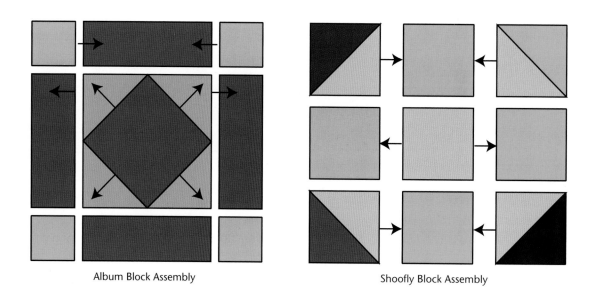

Album Block Assembly

Shoofly Block Assembly

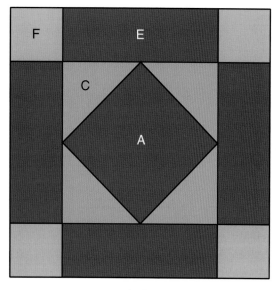

Block 1
make 1

Block 2
make 4

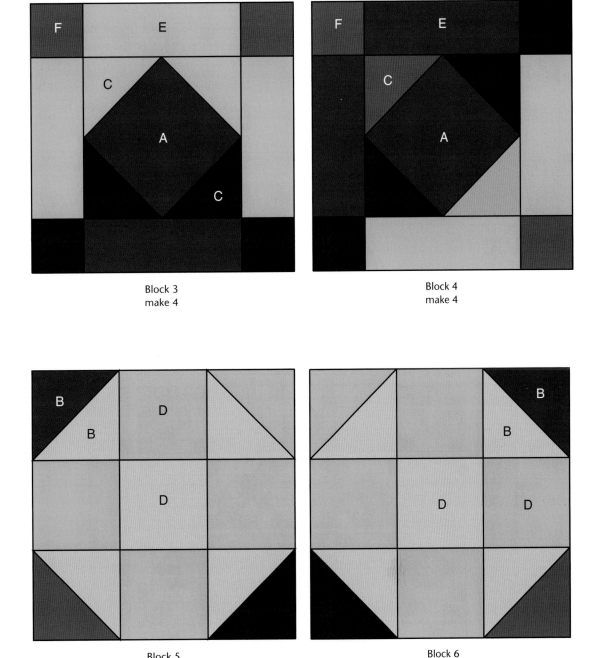

Block 3
make 4

Block 4
make 4

Block 5
make 4

Block 6
make 4

3. Arrange the 25 blocks as shown in the quilt assembly diagram, page 44.
   Join the blocks in each row and press the seam allowances toward the
   Album blocks. Join the rows.

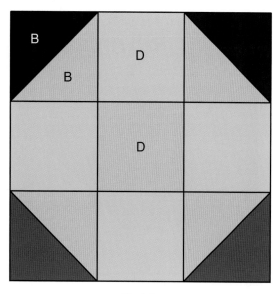

Block 7
make 4

Borders

1. Add the 38" light green strips to the top and bottom of the quilt.

2. Join the 40½" light green strips to the 40½" purple strips. Add these borders to the sides of the quilt.

3. Add the 46½" purple strips to the top and bottom of the quilt.

4. Quilt and bind the layers.

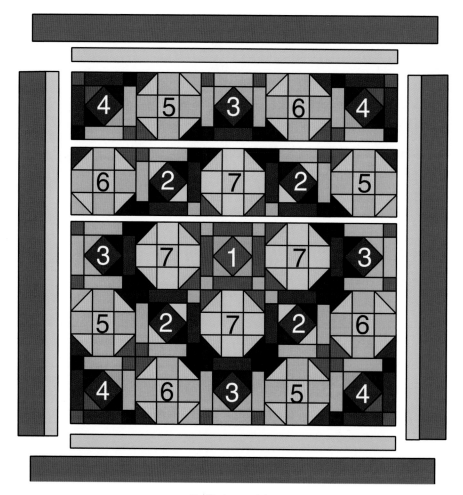

Quilt Assembly

STARS OVER TUCSON

Base block size: 8" • Quilt size: 40" x 48"
Made by Sherall Donovan and quilted by Bonnie Hunter

Sherall Donovan of Tucson, Arizona, started with a Star-in-a-Star block. As she colored the background, she began to see a saguaro cactus. The combination of stars and cactus became STARS OVER TUCSON. The small stars in the central column of the cactus are not horizontally in line with the other stars. When Sherall finished piecing, she said she made a mistake and needed to turn a section of the quilt. I told her it would be easier to just call it a design decision!

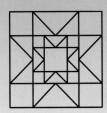

Yardage

Yardage is based on a 40" width.

Placement	Fabric	Yards
Blocks	1	⅝*
	2	1⅛
	3	⅔
	4	¾
	5	¾
Backing		1½
Binding		⅝

*More is needed if the fabric is striped and you want the stripes to be vertical.

Cutting Chart

An "r" indicates that a template needs to be reversed. Templates are on pages 50–51

Shape & Size	Number of Pieces to Cut				
Fabric →	1	2	3	4	5
⊠ A – 5¼"	1 (4)	9 (35)			
☐ B – 4½"	5	7			
T C – template	1	2			
T D – template	1				
☐ E – 3⅜"		26			
◪ F – 2⅞"	3 (5)	2 (3)	4 (8)		89 (178)
T G – template	1&1r	1			
▭ H – 2½" x 38½"	2				
▭ I – 2½" x 10½"	1				
▭ J – 2½" x 6½"	1				
▭ K – 2½" x 4½"	3	22			
☐ L – 2½"	1	10		29	
▭ M – 2½" x 1½"	28		89	1	
◪ N – 1⅞"			2 (4)	2 (4)	
☐ O – 1½"	28		90	234	
T P – template		1			1

Construction

1. The star blocks consist of four Flying Geese units made with the folded corner technique (pages 23–24). There is also one partial star block. Arrows show the seam allowance pressing direction. Make the blocks on the following page.

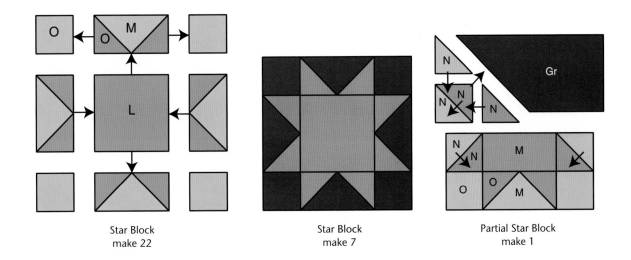

Star Block
make 22

Star Block
make 7

Partial Star Block
make 1

2. Refer to the technique on pages 21–23 to make the Square-in-a-Square block.

3. With templates C and D, make the following units as partial Square-in-a-Square blocks:

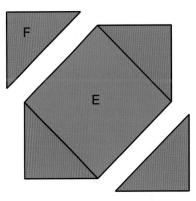

Square-in-a-Square Block
make 26

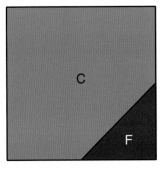

Unit 1
make 2

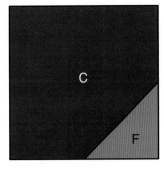

Unit 1
make 1

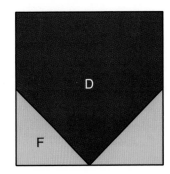

Unit 2
make 1

4. Make the following Flying Geese units:

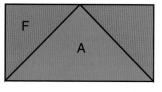

Unit 3
make 35

Unit 3
make 3

Unit 3
make 1

5. Make the following partial geese and half-square triangle units:

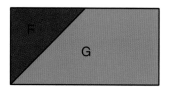

Unit 4
make 1

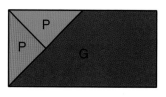

Unit 5
make 1

Unit 6
make 1

Unit 6
make 2

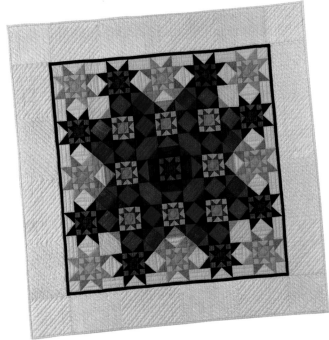

6. Arrange the blocks and units into sections as shown in the quilt assembly diagram, page 49. Join the sections to complete the quilt top.

7. Quilt the layers and bind.

Jeanne Fraser of Tucson, Arizona, also started with the Star-in-a-Star block. Her quilt, SUMMER STARS, is completely different from Sherall's STARS OVER TUCSON.

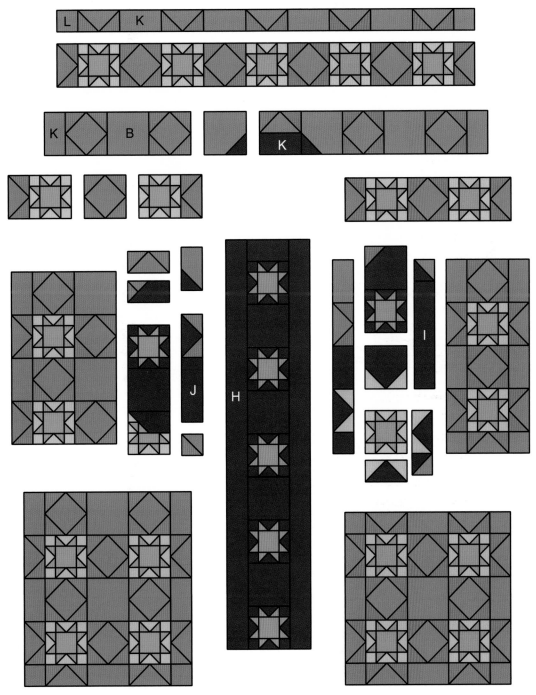

Quilt Assembly

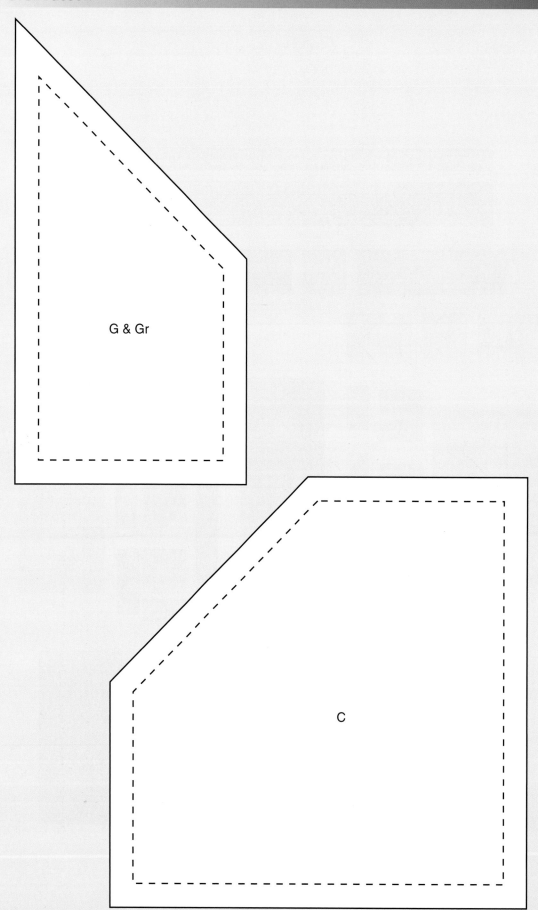

G & Gr

C

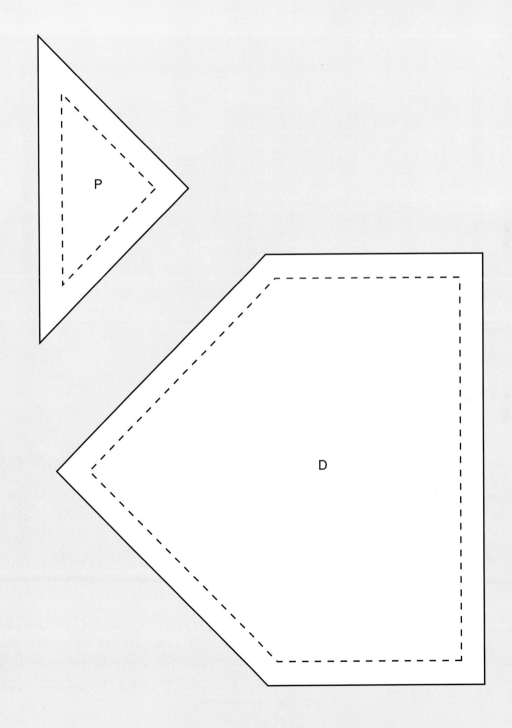

P

D

STARS IN BARS

Base block size: 12" • Quilt size: 56" x 56"
Made by the author and quilted by Terry Clark

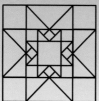

This version of the Star-in-a-Star block includes the added element of a halo behind the smaller star. The background is divided into wide blocks of color and the points of the large stars change color along with the background.

Yardage

Yardage is based on a 40" width.

Placement	Fabric	Yards
Backgrounds	1	½
	2	⅜
	3	⅜
	4	⅜
	5	¾
	6	⅜
	7	⅜
Large star points	8	¼
	9	⅜
	10	⅜
	11	¼
	12	½
Small star	13	½
Halo	14	¼
Inner border		⅜
Outer border & binding		1⅝
Backing		3⅓

Cutting Chart

An "r" indicates that a template needs to be reversed. Templates are on pages 58–60.

Shape & Size	\ Fabric → 1	2	3	4	5	6	7
⊠ A – 7¼"	1 (2)	1 (2)	1 (2)	1 (2)	1 (4)	1 (1)	1 (3)
☐ B – 6½"				1	2		
Ⓣ C – template	2		1			1	
Ⓣ D – template	1					1	
▭ E – 6½" x 3½"		1	1	1	2	1	1
Ⓣ F – template		1r	1				2 & 1r
☐ G – 4¾"	4	1	1	5	10	2	1
◹ H – 3⅞"	2 (3)	1 (1)		2 (4)	3 (6)		1 (1)
☐ I – 3½"	2		1			1	
⊠ J – 2¾"	6 (24)	2 (8)	3 (12)	5 (20)	9 (36)	4 (16)	3 (12)
☐ K – 2"	12	4	6	10	18	8	6

Shape & Size	\ Fabric → 8	9	10	11	12	13	14
◹ H – 3⅞"	6 (12)	12 (24)	18 (36)	4 (8)	24 (48)		
☐ I – 3½"						16	
◺ L – 2⅜"						64 (128)	
☐ M – 1½"							64

Construction

The piecing in this quilt is done in units, not as entire Star-in-a-Star blocks.

1. The small star is pieced the same way every time. The only difference is the background and star point fabrics. Refer to the fabric guide and the quilt assembly guide on page 57 for the correct fabrics as you piece each block.

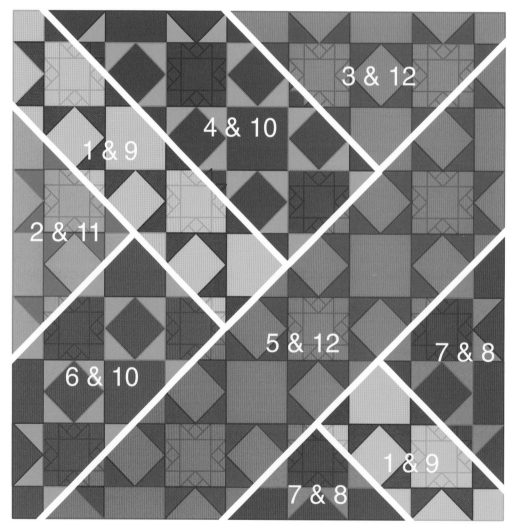

Fabric Guide
Use these fabrics for the background and star points.

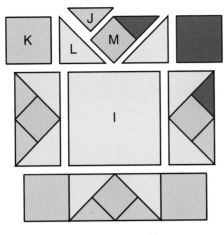

Star Block Assembly

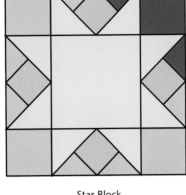

Star Block
make 16
Refer to the fabric guide for the correct colors.

2. The Square-in-a-Square blocks are made from different fabrics. Refer to the fabric guide as you stitch each block. You will be most accurate if you add opposite corners first. When ironing, use a template made from a 6½" muslin square to ensure accuracy without stretching the fabric.

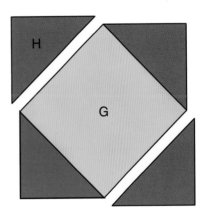

Square-in-a-Square block
make 24
Refer to the fabric guide for the correct colors.

3. There are six partial Square-in-a-Square sections. The ironing template helps keep these accurate as well.

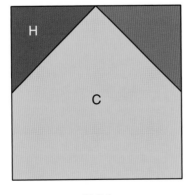

Unit 1
make 4

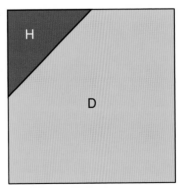

Unit 2
make 2

Refer to the fabric guide for the correct colors.

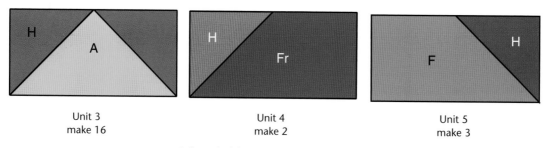

Unit 3
make 16

Unit 4
make 2

Unit 5
make 3

Refer to the fabric guide for the correct colors.

4. The outer edges of the quilt are made of Flying Geese and partial Flying Geese units. A 3½" x 6½" muslin ironing template keeps these sections true to size.

5. Referring to the quilt assembly diagram, join the blocks, units, and other pieces into rows as shown, then join the rows to complete the quilt top.

Borders

1. From the inner border fabric, cut 6 strips 1½" across the fabric width. Join the strips and add them to the sides of the quilt, then to the top and bottom. In a perfect world, the side strips would be cut 48½" and the top and bottom 50½".

2. Measure the quilt top. From the outer border fabric, cut two strips 3½" across the fabric length to equal the measurement. Attach these strips to the sides of the quilt. Measure again for the length of the top and bottom and cut two strips 3½" by this measurement. The side strips should measure 50½" and the top and bottom 56½".

3. Quilt the layers and bind.

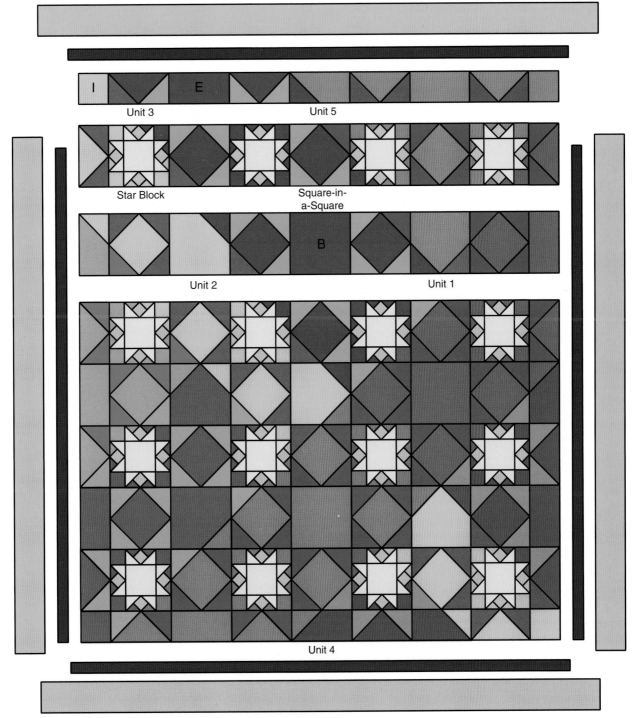

Unit 3

Unit 5

Star Block

Square-in-
a-Square

B

Unit 2

Unit 1

I

E

Unit 4

Quilt Assembly

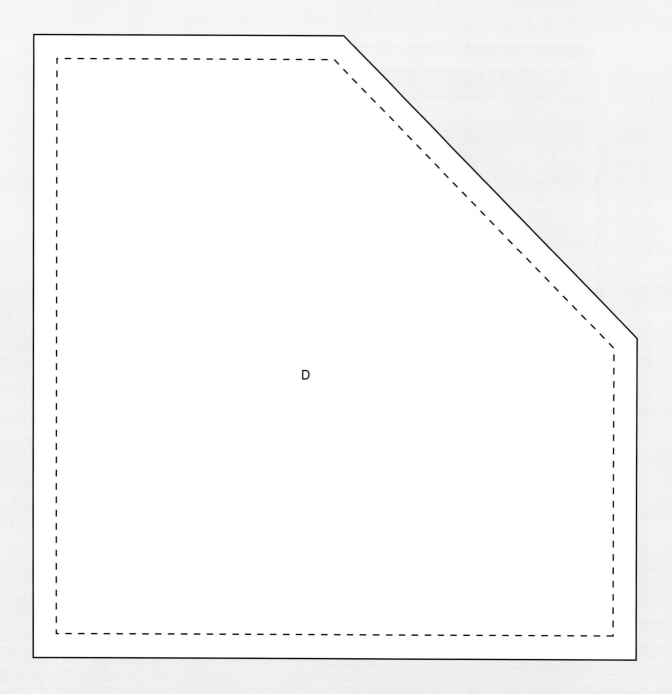

D

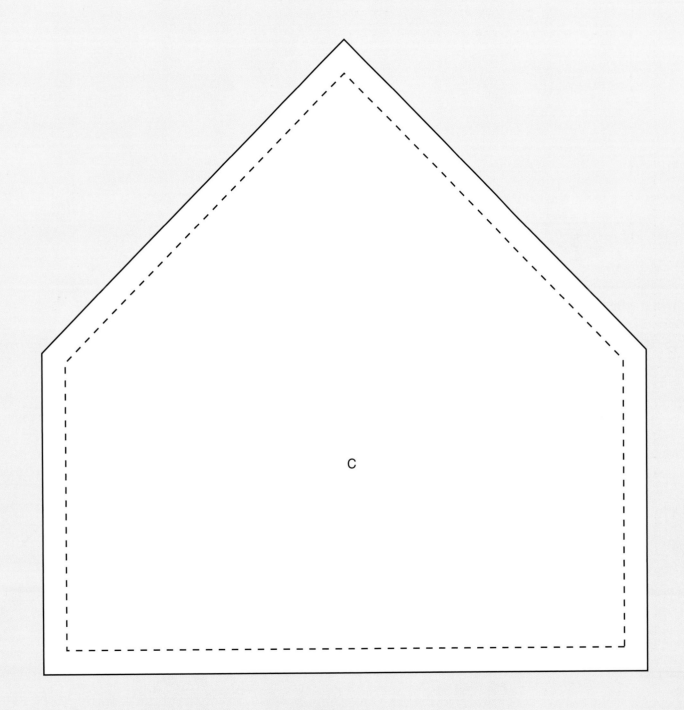

C

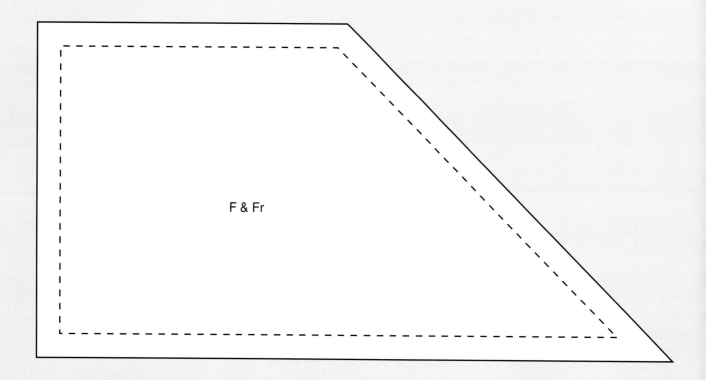

F & Fr

STRETCHING TRADITION

Base block size: 12" • Quilt size: 48" x 60"
Made and quilted by Jo Ann Strohn

Jo Ann Strohn of Tucson, Arizona, started with the Double X block, but it is difficult to find in her completed quilt because many adjacent areas of the block are colored alike. She used 20 blocks and rotated every other one by 90°. She added some new lines across the surface of the quilt and began coloring.

The project directions have slightly simplified her quilt by using just one yellow fabric in the center section instead of three.

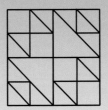

Yardage

Yardage is based on a 40" width.

Placement	Fabric	Yards
Sections	1	¾
	2	¾
	3	1
	4	⅛
	5	⅜
	6	½
	7	⅛
	8	¾
	9	⅛
	10	⅛
	11	⅝
Backing		3*
Binding		⅝

*crosswise seam

Cutting Chart

An "r" indicates that a template needs to be reversed. Templates on pages 66–69.

Shape & Size	Number of Pieces to Cut										
Fabric →	1	2	3	4	5	6	7	8	9	10	11
⊠ A – 7¼"	1 (1)		1 (2)			1 (4)		1 (4)			1 (4)
◺ B – 6⅞"	7 (13)	7 (13)	7 (13)		2 (3)			2 (3)			3 (6)
Ⓣ C – template					1			1			
☐ D – 4¾" x 13¼"	2										
☐ E – 4¾"		1				1		1			
◺ F – 3⅞"	1 (1)		1 (1)	5 (9)		6 (11)	2 (4)	2 (3)	2 (4)	2 (4)	2 (4)
Ⓣ G – template			1 & 1r								
Ⓣ H – template	2 & 1r				1			1 & 1r			1 & 1r
☐ I – 3½" x 6½"		2									1
☐ J – 3½"	10	9	12		4			4			5
Ⓣ K – template						1					
Ⓣ L – template			8			1		1			1
☐ M – 2⅝" x 13¼"						2		2			2
Ⓣ N – template		8						4			1
☐ O – 2⅝" x 9"						2		2			2

The piecing for this quilt appears fairly complicated, but isn't if you stay organized. To help, label 15 small plastic bags with the letters of the shapes and place the pieces in the appropriate bag as they are cut. It will be easier to find the pieces for each section if they are sorted as soon as they are cut.

This quilt is constructed in sections, then the sections are joined. Handle the outside edges gently because there are a few places where the outer grain line is on the bias.

Construction

1. Find the pieces for one section at a time. The sewing order for each section is up to you. Most of the piecing will be fairly obvious after it is laid out. Join smaller triangles to make larger ones, or to make squares and rectangles. The sections have been chosen so that the piecing will be easy. Continue constructing the sections one at a time. Make the following sections:

Section 1

B – 5 of fabric 2, 3 of fabric 11

H – 1 of fabric 11

J – 4 of fabric 2, 4 of fabric 11

Section 2

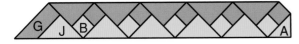

A – 1 of fabric 1

B – 5 of fabric 3, 5 of fabric 1

G – 1 of fabric 3

J – 5 of fabric 3, 5 of fabric 1

Section 3

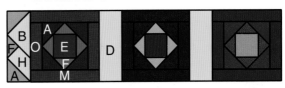

A – 4 of fabric 8, 4 of fabric 11,
4 of fabric 6, 2 of fabric 3

B – 1 of fabric 1

D – 2 of fabric 1

E – 1 of fabric 2, 1 of fabric 8,
1 of fabric 6

F – 4 of fabric 7, 4 of fabric 9,
4 of fabric 10, 1 of fabric 3

H – 1 of fabric 1

M – 2 of fabric 8, 2 of fabric 11,
2 of fabric 6

O – 2 of fabric 8, 2 of fabric 11,
2 of fabric 6

Section 4

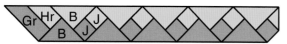

B – 5 of fabric 3, 5 of fabric 1
F – 1 of fabric 1
G – 1r of fabric 3
H – 1r of fabric 1
J – 5 of fabric 3, 4 of fabric 1

Section 5

B – 1 of fabric 2, 2 of fabric 1,
    1 of fabric 3
H – 1 of fabric 1
J – 2 of fabric 3, 1 of fabric 1

Section 6

F – 1 of fabric 6
L – 1 of fabric 11
N – 1 of fabric 8

Section 7

B – 2 of fabric 11
F – 1 of fabric 6, 1 of fabric 8
I – 1 of fabric 11, 1 of fabric 2
N – 1 of fabric 8, 1 of fabric 11

Section 8

B – 2 of fabric 3, 2 of fabric 2, 1 of fabric 11
F – 1 of fabric 6
H – 1r of fabric 11
I – 1 of fabric 2
J – 1 of fabric 2, 1 of fabric 11

Section 9

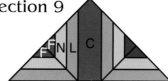

C – 1 of fabric 5
F – 2 of fabric 11, 2 of fabric 6
L – 4 of fabric 3
N – 4 of fabric 2

Section 10

B – 3 of fabric 5
F – 9 of fabric 4
H – 1 of fabric 5
J – 4 of fabric 5

Section 11

F – 4 of fabric 6, 2 of fabric 8
H – 1r of fabric 8
K – 1 of fabric 6
L – 1 of fabric 8, 1 of fabric 6
N – 2 of fabric 8

Section 12

B – 5 of fabric 2, 3 of fabric 8
H – 1 of fabric 8
J – 4 of fabric 2, 4 of fabric 8

Section 13

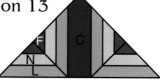

C – 1 of fabric 8
F – 2 of fabric 11, 2 of fabric 6
L – 4 of fabric 3
N – 4 of fabric 2

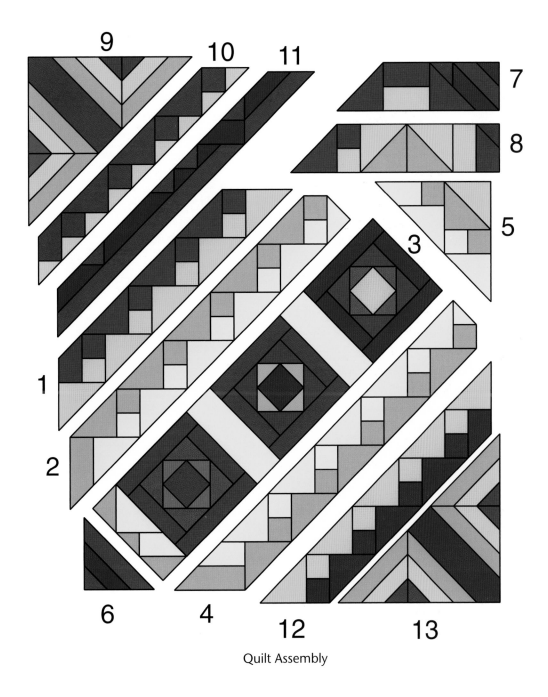

Quilt Assembly

2. Once the sections have been pieced, join sections 1, 2, 3, and 4. Add 5 and 6 to the ends of the pieced sections. Join 7 and 8 and add to the pieced sections. Join 9, 10, and 11 and add to the pieced sections. Join 12 and 13 and add to the rest of the quilt top.

3. Quilt the layers and bind.

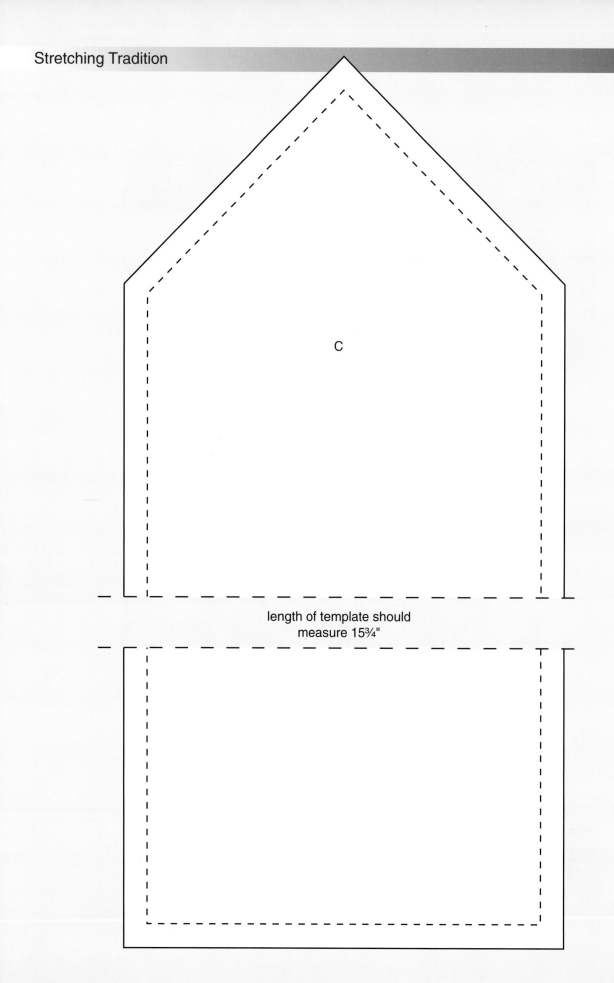

C

length of template should
measure 15¾"

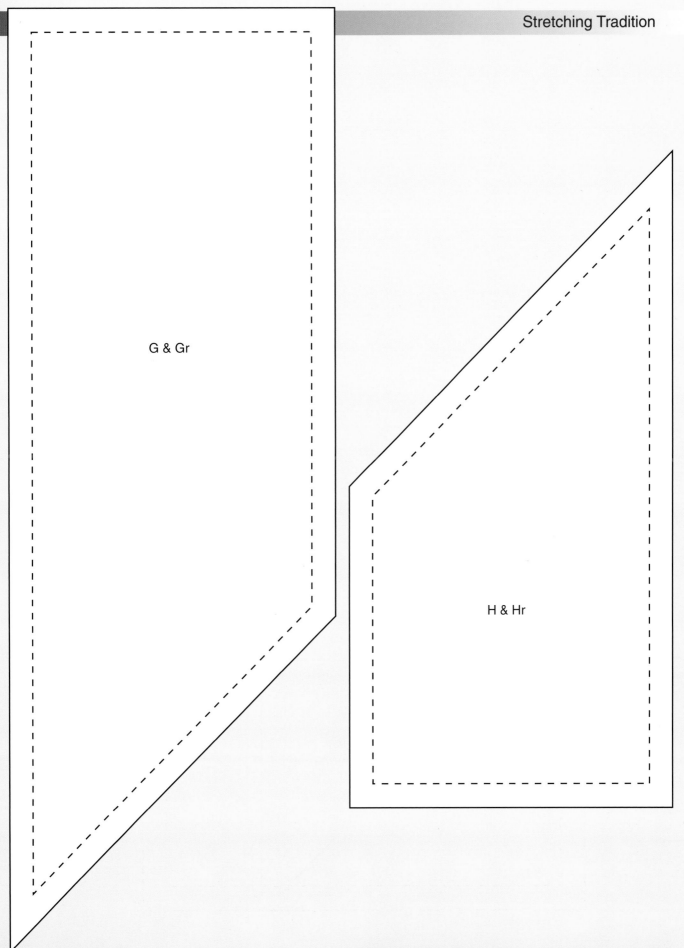

G & Gr

H & Hr

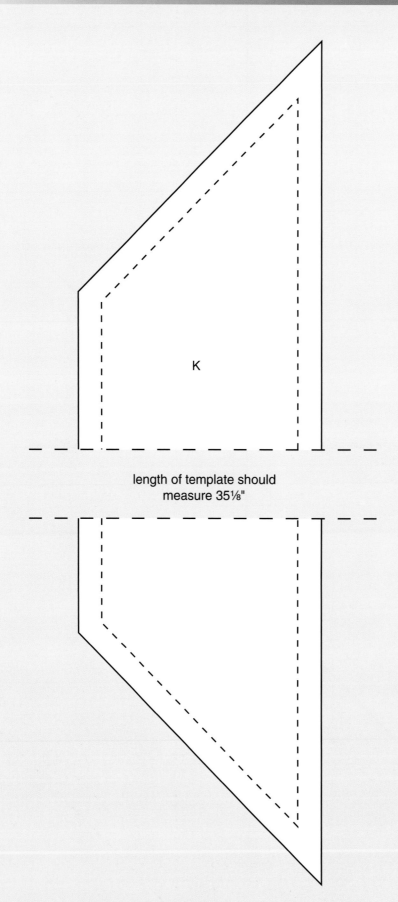

K

length of template should
measure 35⅛"

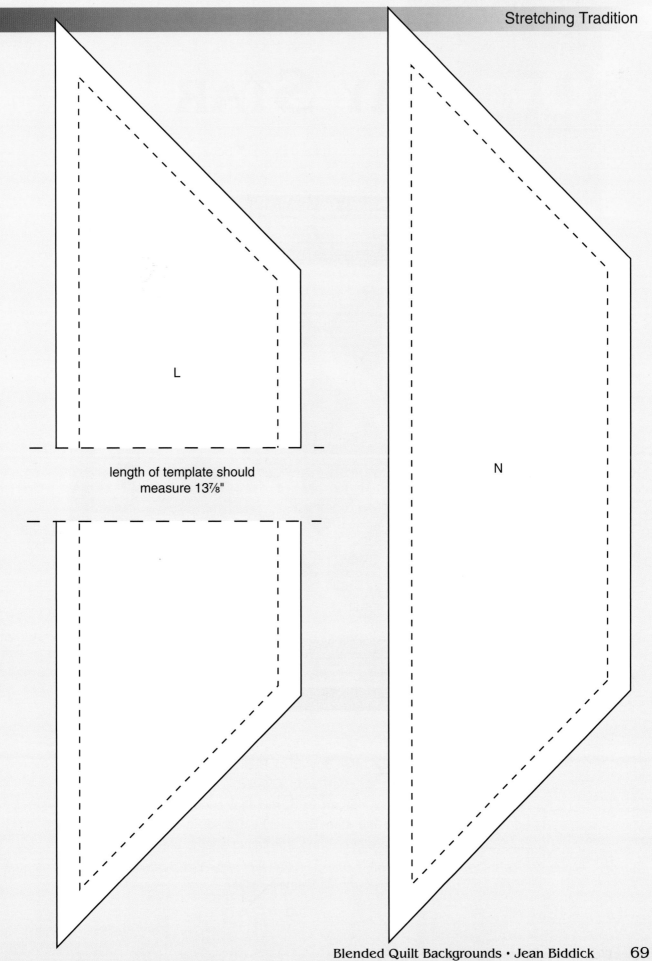

L

length of template should
measure 13⅞"

N

OVERLAY STAR

Base block size: 12" • Quilt size: 49" x 49"
Made and quilted by Kathy Bower

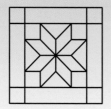

Kathy Bower of Berkeley Heights, New Jersey, started with a Variable Star block. Her version includes an extra row that effectively adds a border to the star. The blocks are set in a 3 x 3 grid. With careful coloring, she found a large star superimposed on the grid. The result is one large star overlaid on a background of smaller stars.

Yardage

Yardage is based on a 40" width. The fabrics in this quilt consist of light, medium and dark shades of colors teal, gold, and green.

	Placement	Fabric	Yards
	Units & sections	lt	½
		med	½
		dk	⅜
		lt	⅜
	Units, sections & pieced border	med	1
		dk	¼
		lt	¼
		med	⅝
		dk	¼
	Border & binding		1½
	Backing		3

Cutting Chart for the Quilt Body

An "r" indicates that a template needs to be reversed. Templates are on page 75.

Shape & Size		Number of Pieces to Cut								
Fabric →	lt	med	dk	lt	med	dk	lt	med	dk
⊠ A – 9¼"		1 (4)							
☐ B – 8½" x 2½"	12	8	8						
⊠ C – 5¼"	4 (16)	3 (12)	2 (8)						
◩ D – 4⅞"	4 (8)			2 (4)					
◩ E – 2⅞"				20 (40)	8 (16)	16 (32)			
☐ F – 2½"				8	8	4			
T G – template							16 & 16r	12 & 12r	8 & 8r

Construction

Find the pieces for one section at a time. Follow the assembly diagrams and lay out the pieces for those sections. See the quilt assembly diagram, page 75, to see where each section is used in the quilt.

1. To make Unit 1, use Y-seam construction to join the diamond templates to the triangles, placing the long diamond edge next to the triangle. Refer to the diagram on page 72 to make four of Unit 1.

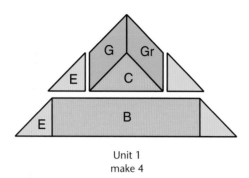

Unit 1 – make 4

B – 1 light teal

C – 1 light teal

E – 4 light gold

G – 1 & 1r light green

Unit 1
make 4

2. Refer to the following diagram to make four of Unit 2. Add the center F square to the edges of template G, then close the seam between the diamonds.

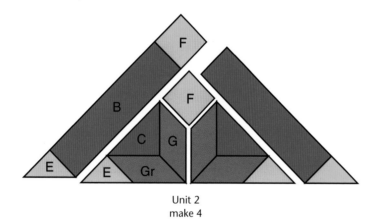

Unit 2 – make 4

B – 2 medium teal

C – 2 medium teal

E – 4 medium gold

F – 2 medium gold

G – 2 & 2r medium green

Unit 2
make 4

3. Refer to the following diagram to make four middle sections, which are constructed by adding Unit 1 to each side of Unit 2. Note the changes in color.

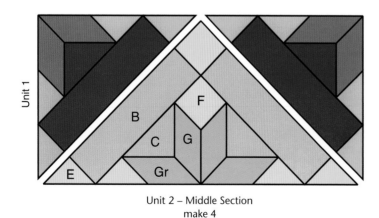

Middle Section – make 4

B – 2 light teal, 2 dark teal

C – 2 light teal, 2 dark teal

E – 4 light gold, 8 dark gold

F – 2 light gold

G – 2 & 2r light green,
2 & 2r dark green

Unit 2 – Middle Section
make 4

4. Make one center section following the diagram. Start by constructing the diamond units and adding an F square to the right side of each unit. Close the seam between the F and the diamond first, then between the two diamonds. Join the center seam in the same manner.

Center Section – make 1
A – 4 medium teal
C – 4 light teal, 4 medium teal
D – 8 light teal, 4 light gold
E – 8 light gold
F – 4 medium gold
G – 4 & 4r light green, 4 & 4r medium green

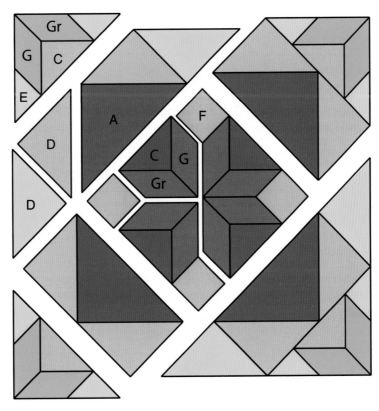

Center Section
make 1

5. Join the units and sections as shown in the quilt assembly diagram, page 75, to complete the quilt top.

Borders
Cutting Chart for the Border

Measure the quilt body for accuracy before cutting the border strips. For the inner border, cut two strips 2¼" x 36½" and two strips 2¼" x 40½". For the outer border, cut two strips 2½" x 45½" and two strips 2½" x 49½".

Shape & Size	Number of Pieces to Cut	
Fabric →		
⊠ H – 6⅞"	6 (24)	
◺ I – 6½"	2 (4)	
⊠ J – 3¼"	14 (56)	
◺ K – 1⅞"	28 (56)	
☐ L – 1½"	28	
Ⓣ M – template		56 & 56r

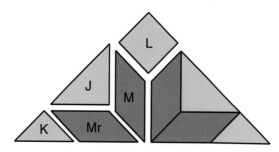

Half-Star Unit

Border Assembly

1. Make 28 half-star units. Join seven half-star units alternately with six H triangles. Make four of pieced borders.

2. Sew the inner border strips to the sides, then to the top and bottom of the quilt.

3. Add the pieced sections to each side of the quilt. Complete the pieced border using the four I triangles.

4. Sew the outer border strips to the sides, then to the top and bottom of the quilt.

5. Quilt the layers and bind.

Quilt Assembly

G & Gr

Start with a 2½" strip.

M & Mr

Start with a 1½" strip.

FIRE STORM

Quilt size: 60" x 75"
Made by Gayle Strack and quilted by Nubin Jensen

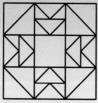

Gayle Strack of Tucson, Arizona, used the Cut the Corners block, also known as Double T, for her quilt. She set the blocks on point in a 4 x 5 grid. Instead of a block size, this quilt is based on a 2½" unit.

Yardage

Yardage is based on a 40" width.

Placement	Fabric	Yards
Quilt sections	1	¾
	2	⅜
	3	1¾
	4	¾
	5	1
	6	⅜
	7	1¾
	8	⅝
	9	1½
Backing		3⅝
Binding		¾

Cutting Chart

Shape & Size	Number of Pieces to Cut								
Fabric →	1	2	3	4	5	6	7	8	9
☒ A – 6¼"	4 (16)	1 (2)	23 (91)	5 (19)	7 (28)	6 (24)	26 (102)	4 (15)	1 (1)
☐ B – 4"	9	1	8	6	8				
☒ C – 3¾"							54 (216)	30 (120)	76 (304)
◤ D – 3⅜"	12 (24)	6 (12)	47 (93)	15 (30)	22 (43)	4 (8)	10 (20)	3 (6)	1 (2)
☐ E – 3"	12	2	36	12	17				

Construction

1. The colors in this quilt change in sections. There are eight different fabric combinations. Use the fabric guide on page 78 to determine the correct fabrics for each section. Refer to both the fabric guide and quilt assembly diagram to lay out the pieces for the quilt top.

2. The piecing is done in diagonal rows, which alternate between wide and narrow bands. The units in each row are made up of half-square triangle pairs, Square-in-a-Square units, and Flying Geese. Refer to the piecing tips on pages 21–24 for construction details.

3. Refer to the quilt assembly diagram, page 79, to join the units to form the diagonal rows. Join the rows to form the quilt top.

4. Quilt and bind the layers.

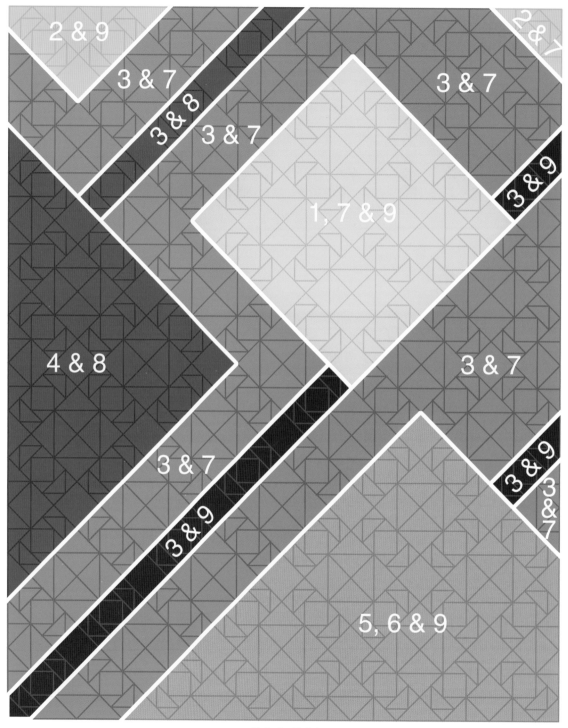

Fabric Guide
Use these fabrics for the background and units.

Quilt Assembly

TOUCHED BY THE SUN

Base block size: 10" • Quilt size: 62" x 72"
Made by Jo Cady-Bull and quilted by Mary Vaneecke

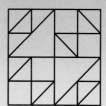

The sun shines through leafy trees and ends up as patches of light in this quilt by Jo Cady-Bull of Tucson, Arizona. Her quilt started with the Old Maid's Puzzle block. She added diagonal lines through parts of the background and the colors in the resulting bands weave over and under each other.

Yardage

Yardage is based on a 40" width.

Placement	Fabric	Yards
Quilt sections	1	¾
	2	¼
	3	⅝
	4	⅞
	5	⅝
	6	½
Inner border	7	1
	8	1½
Outer border & binding		2
Backing*		3⅔

*crosswise seam

Cutting Chart

Before cutting the following pieces, cut seven strips 1½" across the width of the blue fabric for the inner border. An "r" indicates that a template needs to be reversed. Templates are on pages 85–87.

Shape & Size	1	2	3	4	5	6	7	8
⊠ A – 6¼"			1 (1)	1 (1)	1 (1)			1 (1)
◹ B – 5⅞"								30 (59)
T C – template	2			1				
T D – template	1		1	2	1	2		
⊠ E – 3¾"	3 (10)	1 (4)	1 (4)	2 (6)	3 (9)	2 (7)		
◹ F – 3⅜"	10 (19)	4 (8)	11 (22)	10 (20)	7 (14)	3 (6)	60 (120)	30 (60)
T G – template	6 & 7r		3 & 5r	7 & 7r	5 & 5r	3 & 4r		
T H – template					1			
☐ I – 3"	5	4	4	7	4	3		
T J – template	2 & 1r		1r	3 & 2r	2 & 3r	1 & 1r		
T K – template	1r		1 & 2r	2 & 1r	2 & 2r	1 & 1r		
T L – template	7 & 6r		5 & 3r	7 & 7r	5 & 5r	3 & 4r		
▭ M – 2¼" x 4"	1		1	1	1			
☐ N – 2¼"	3		2		1	4		

Construction

1. The quilt is constructed in diagonal rows. Refer to the background fabric guide, page 82, to see where the different background fabrics are used.

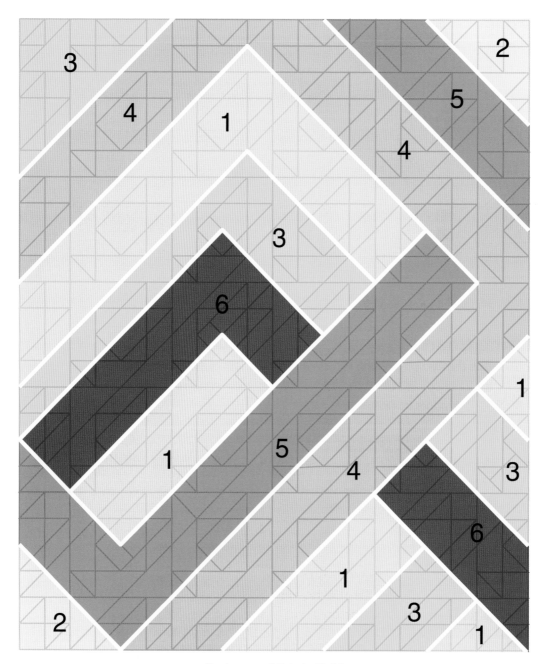

Background Fabric Guide

2. The main units in each row are pieced as parallelograms. To construct these units, start in the center with piece C. As pieces are added, press the seams away from the center. The center of the block is not always made from a single C template. The row assembly diagrams illustrate several variations.

3. At the edges of each diagonal row are side blocks. The following illustration shows the basic construction of these blocks.

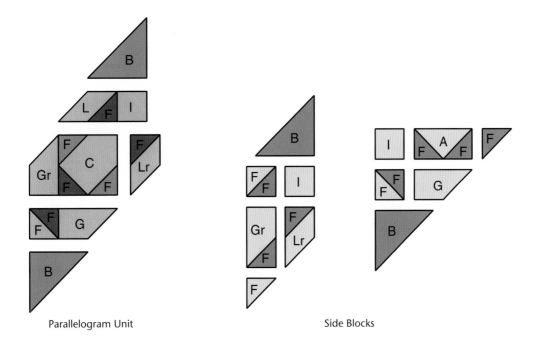

Parallelogram Unit   Side Blocks

4. Construct each row following the row assembly diagrams, and note the background color changes. After constructing each row, join the rows to each other following the quilt assembly diagram, page 84.

Borders

1. For the inner border, join two blue strips for each of the quilts sides. Cut them to size and attach the side borders. Join one and a half strips each for the top and bottom of the quilt, cut to size, and attach to the quilt.

2. For the outer border, cut four strips 5½" x 62½" across the length of the border fabric. Add the strips to the sides of the quilt, then to the top and bottom.

3. Quilt and bind the layers.

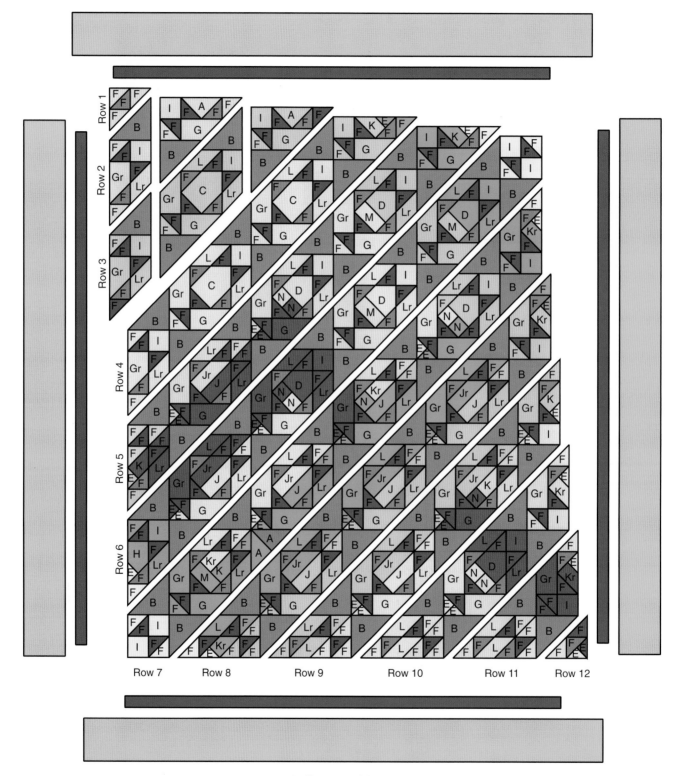

Quilt Assembly

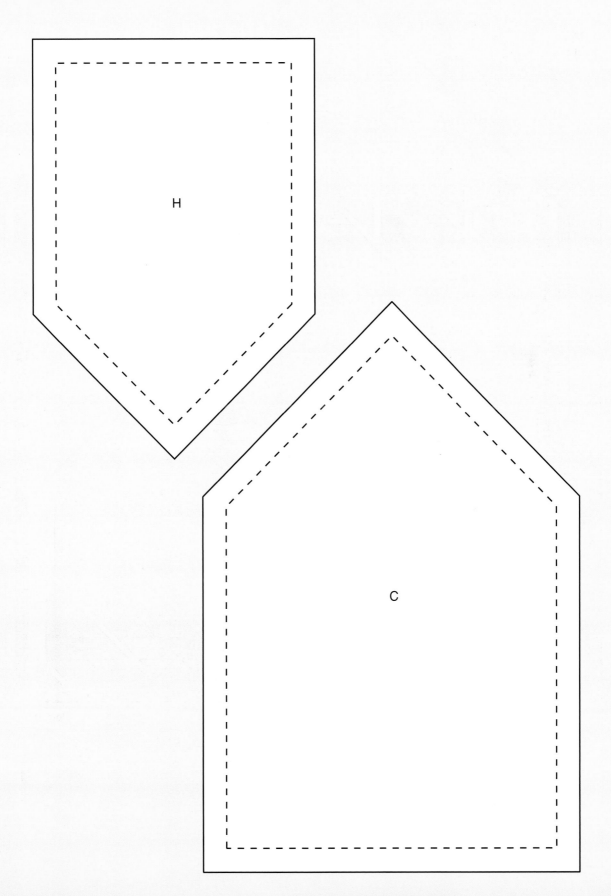

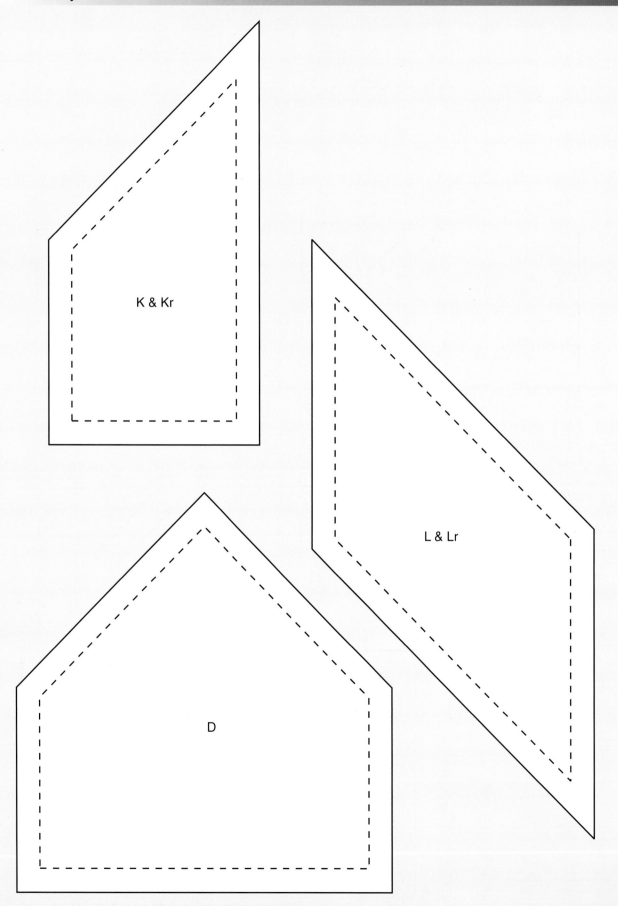

K & Kr

L & Lr

D

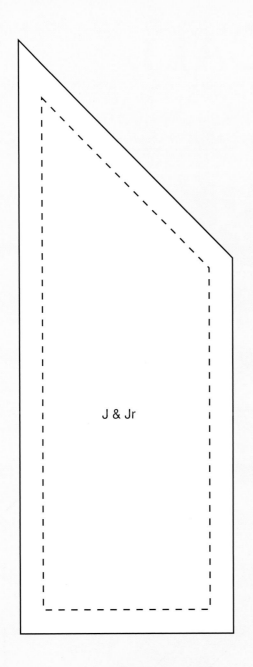

J & Jr

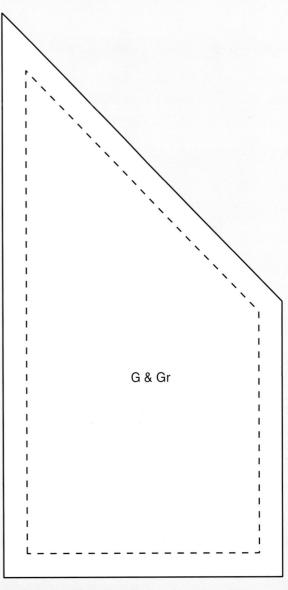

G & Gr

CURTAIN CALL

Base block size : 9" • Quilt size: 51" x 69"
Made by the author and quilted by Jo Lee Hazelwood

 King's Crown and Arkansas Snowflake blocks are set alternately in a 5 x 7 grid. The corners repeat the King's Crown block instead of continuing the alternating pattern.

Yardage

Yardage is based on a 40" width.

Placement	Fabric	Yards
Blocks	1	¾
	2	⅞
	3	¼
	4	1¼
	5	¾
	6	1¼
	7	⅓
Border & binding		1⅞
Backing*		3⅛

*crosswise seam

Cutting Chart

Cut lengthwise strips for the borders. Cut two strips 3½" x 63½" and two strips 3½" x 51½". Reserve the rest for binding. An "r" indicates a template that needs to be reversed. Templates are on page 94.

Shape & Size	Number of Pieces to Cut						
Fabric →	1	2	3	4	5	6	7
⊠ A – 5¾"	9 (34)	3 (12)		6 (22)		4 (16)	
◩ B – 5⅜"		2 (4)		2 (4)	2 (4)	14 (28)	
T C – template				14 & 14r			
☐ D – 5"	7	14					
⊠ E – 4¼"		1 (4)				3 (10)	4 (14)
T F – template			4 & 4r	16 & 16r	16 & 16r		
◩ G – 3⅞"		2 (4)				5 (10)	
T H – template						6	14
T I – template		4 & 4r				12 & 12r	
☐ J – 3½"			8	16	32	4	
◩ K – 3⅛"	16 (32)	14 (28)					
☐ L – 2¾"						16	

Construction

The blocks in this quilt are constructed traditionally, then sewn into rows.

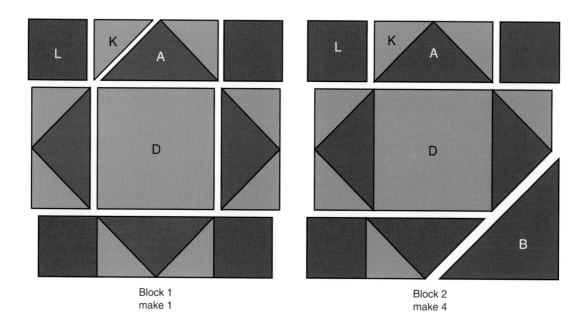

Block 1
make 1

Block 2
make 4

1. For block 1, make four Flying Geese sections, then use basic Nine-Patch construction to complete the block.

2. For block 2, make two Flying Geese sections and two half geese. Press the seam allowances toward the L squares on the top row. On the second row, press the seam allowances toward the center D, then toward L on the third row. Join the rows and add B.

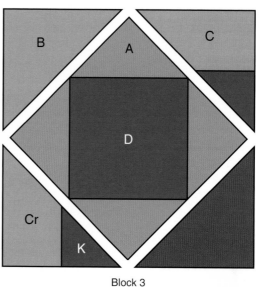

Block 3
make 4

3. For block 3, start by making the Square-in-a-Square unit in the center. Then, join C and Cr to a K triangle. Add these units to opposite sides of the center unit, then add B to the other two corners.

4. Blocks 4, 5, and 6 have different colorings, but their construction is the same. Press the seam allowances toward C and Cr on the top row. For the center section, join A and K and press the seam allowance toward K. Make two of these units and add them to the opposites sides of D. Join the top row to the center section. Add A to the bottom edge of the completed

section and press the seam allowance toward A. Add two B triangles to the bottom corners and press toward B.

5. Block 7 is pieced as a traditional Square-in-a-Square block.

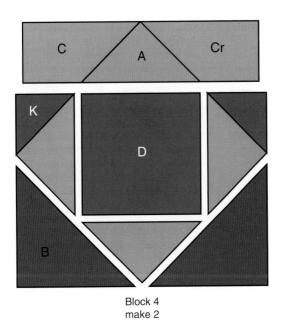

Block 4
make 2

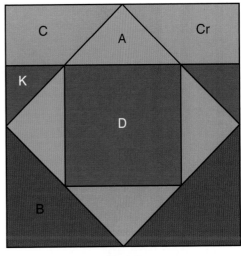

Block 5
make 4

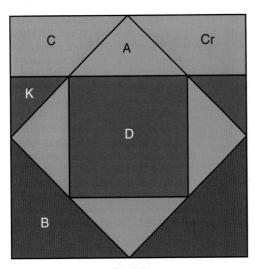

Block 6
make 4

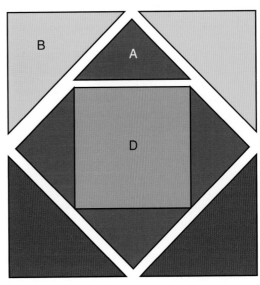

Block 7
make 2

6. The Arkansas Snowflake block has four variations. When constructing the center, press the seam toward the green E piece, then toward the G piece. For the sides of the block, press all seams toward the F pieces. Construct the following blocks:

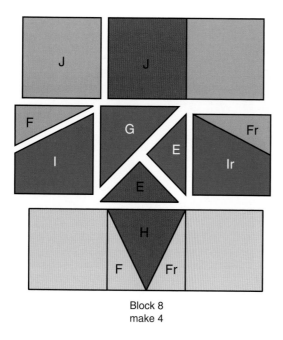

Block 8
make 4

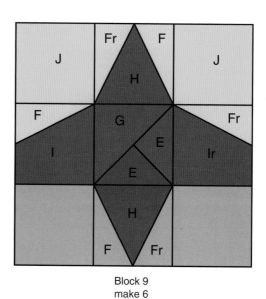

Block 9
make 6

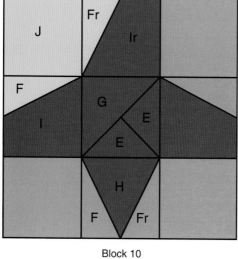

Block 10
make 2

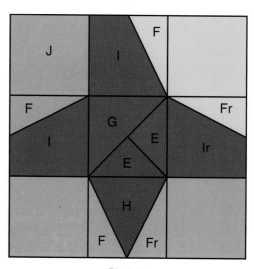

Block 11
make 2

6. Refer to the quilt assembly diagram to lay out the blocks. Join the blocks into rows, then join the rows to each other.

7. Sew the borders to the sides of the quilt, then to the top and bottom.

8. Quilt the layers and bind.

Quilt Assembly

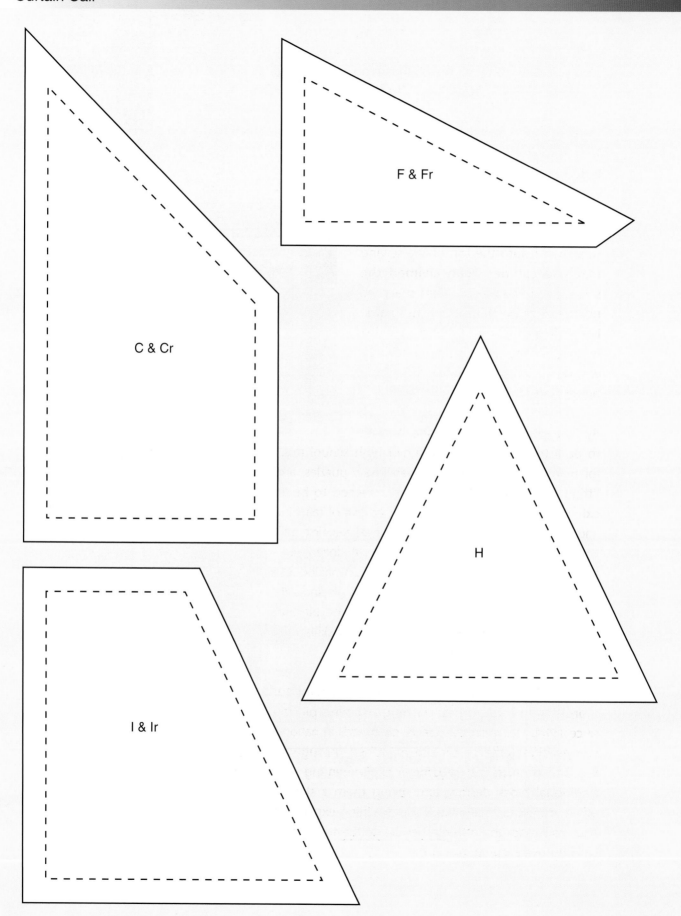

C & Cr

F & Fr

H

I & Ir

ABOUT THE AUTHOR

Two things should have given Jean Biddick an early hint that quilting was in her future. First, when she was four years old, her mother taught her to print her name and she promptly scratched it into the top of the sewing machine cabinet. Jean claimed the sewing machine early. That machine now lives at her house and her name is still faintly visible. Second, the first house Jean and her husband purchased was on Calico Street. What could be a better start for a quilter?

By first grade, Jean knew she wanted to be a teacher. She taught junior high school math for many years. Another love was jigsaw puzzles, and fitting together small bits of fabric seemed to be an extension of that love. Combining her love of teaching and piecing came naturally. Jean started her first quilt (still unfinished) in junior high school. A dozen years later, she became more serious about quiltmaking and was introduced to machine piecing. Jean's piecing skills improved and she began teaching machine piecing. She enjoys giving students the technical skills they need to turn their vision into quilts.

Jean has been piecing traditional quilt patterns for more than 30 years and teaching machine piecing since 1984. Her quilts have received awards in national competitions and have been exhibited throughout the United States. She has been experimenting with traditional block designs and giving them a slightly different look for many years. Her teaching experience and math background help her clarify the things that can improve accurate piecing.

OTHER AQS BOOKS

This is only a small selection of the books available from the American Quilter's Society. AQS books are known worldwide for timely topics, clear writing, beautiful color photos, and accurate illustrations and patterns. The following books are available from your local bookseller, quilt shop, or public library.

FABRIC *Fandango*
Combining Hand-Dyed and Commercial Prints
Gail Simpson
#7490   us$22.95

ONE-DERFUL 1 Fabric Quilts
Kay Nickols
#7487   us$18.95

Celtic PIECED ILLUSIONS
KAREN COMBS
#7014   us$24.95

QUILTS for Ice Cream Lovers
Janet Jones Worley
#7075   us$21.95

NINE-PATCH *Extravaganza*
JUDY L. LAQUIDARA
#7484   us$22.95

Scallops Sew EASY
Marie Seroskie
#7486   us$19.95

QUILTED ONE BLOCK MARVELS
CAROLYN SULLIVAN
#7491   us$22.95

Quilt Mavens Perfect Paper Piecing
DEB KARASIK JANET MEDNICK
#7018   us$24.95

MYSTERY QUILTS
RITA FISHEL
#7079   us$22.95

Look for these books nationally. **1-800-626-5420**
Call or **Visit** our Web site at **www.AmericanQuilter.com**